THE DRAMA OF THE PSALMS

Donald Anders-Richards

THE DRAMA
OF THE PSALMS

Judson Press, Valley Forge

First published in 1968 by
Darton, Longman & Todd Ltd
85 Gloucester Road, London S.W.7
© 1968 Donald Anders-Richards

Published by Judson Press 1970

Standard Book No. 8170-0478-5
Library of Congress Catalog Card No. 79-100965

TO M. AND D.
IN GRATITUDE

Reproduced and Printed in Great Britain by
Redwood Press Limited, Trowbridge & London.

CONTENTS

ACKNOWLEDGEMENTS

The author would like to acknowledge his special indebtedness, both in respect of knowledge and inspiration, to the works of Professor A. R. Johnson, formerly of University College, Cardiff.

The Scripture quotations in this publication are from the *Revised Standard Version of the Bible* copyrighted 1946 and 1952 and used by permission.

CHAPTER ONE

A First Look at the Psalms

JUST ABOUT 400 YEARS AGO, THE SIXTEENTH century theologian Richard Hooker wrote this about the psalms:

> The choice and flower of all things profitable in other books the Psalms do both more briefly contain, and more movingly express. . . . What is there necessary for man to know which the Psalms are not able to teach? They are to beginners an easy and familiar introduction, a mighty augmentation of all virtue and knowledge in such as are entered before, a strong confirmation to the most perfect amongst others. Heroical magnanimity, exquisite justice, grave moderation, exact wisdom, repentance unfeigned, unwearied patience, the mysteries of God, the sufferings of Christ, the terrors of wrath, the comforts of grace, the works of providence over this world, and the promised joys of that world which is to come, all good necessarily to be either known or done or had, this one celestial fountain yieldeth. . . . Hereof it is that we covet to make the Psalms especially familiar unto all (*Laws of Ecclesiastical Polity*, Bk. V, 37. 2).

It is not unreasonable to suggest that the great majority of Christians today still share Hooker's view of the psalms, albeit expressed in simpler terms. For them the psalms are the expression of the outpouring of the individual's soul to God, the revelation of his inmost thoughts in moments of great spiritual significance.

That this should in fact be the general outlook on the psalms is not really surprising considering the use which the 'churches' of God have made of them. For several hundred years, for example, in the daily services of both Christian and Jewish communities, the psalms have held a place of their own. The Christian church uses them in a supporting role in daily services in addition to the set portion of the Book of Psalms which is prescribed for recital each day. Then too in both marriage and burial services appropriate psalms are said or sung, and much use of them is made in private devotion. In fact the Book of Psalms has assumed quite naturally and rightly, the status of a 'Prayer book' in its own right, and the general reader tends therefore to see it as a collection of prayers to be made his own, and to be used as occasion demands for the expression of deeply spiritual thoughts and attitudes of mind concerning his relationship to God.

Of course there is nothing at all wrong with the adoption of the Psalter as a personal prayer-book! What is important is that something of the true historical origin of the psalms should be understood, not merely because they form such a great part of our religious heritage, but because knowledge and understanding of the real-life situation from which individual psalms spring, renders them so much the more valuable spiritually and devotionally.

Can it then be stated with any great degree of accuracy, what was the true historical origin of the psalms? The answer to this crucial question is to be found in the writings of scholars over a period of some 2,000 years, but it is in the past 100 years that psalm study has really come into its own. The brief summary which follows, sets down the generally accepted conclusions about the Book of Psalms which have been reached during this latter period of intensive work and study.

A typical quotation, which offers a guide to the climate of

opinion about the psalms early in the present century, is from C. F. Kent's book, *The Songs, Hymns and Prayers of the Old Testament* (1914). The author writes: 'Thus the evidence is conclusive that the Psalter has a history as long and complex as the Old Testament itself. Certain of its older poems may come from the days of David, about 1000 B.C. Its later psalms breathe the warlike spirit of the Maccabean age. It represents the growth of at least eight centuries and the work of fully 100 poets. Behind it lie two millenniums of Semitic religious history; but the Psalms themselves, with few exceptions, come from the four centuries and a half which began with the destruction of Jerusalem in 586 B.C. They record the inspired insight, the dauntless courage, and the profound spiritual experiences of the noble souls who faced the cruel persecutions and the great crises of the Persian, Greek and Maccabean periods. Born in stress and struggle, they have a unique message and meaning for all who are in the stream of life.'

Here Kent is expressing a conventional view of the psalms which was that of his own generation and of most commentators who had gone before him. It is difficult to imagine that he could have foreseen or indeed understood the vastly different view of the Psalter which is accepted today. The purpose of this book is to set out and account for remarkable developments in this field, but in order that the extent of these developments may be fully appreciated, it is first of all necessary to survey the older traditional pattern of psalm study.

If this traditional method of approach to the psalms is to be given a designation, it could well be called the historical and biographical approach. Each psalm was considered as an individual composition, and its character and date was decided almost entirely on the subject matter which it contained. The commentary of A. F. Kirkpatrick, which is used in detail in Chapter Four, is a classic example of this method of approach. For instance, looking at *Psalm* 132, Kirkpatrick has this to say (in brief):

Remember, O Lord, in David's favour, all the hardships he
   endured;
How he swore to the Lord and vowed to the Mighty One of Jacob,
'I will not enter my house or get into my bed; I will not give sleep
   to my eyes or slumber to my eyelids, until I find a place for the
   Lord, a dwelling place for the Mighty One of Jacob'

(vvs.1–5)

The first five verses of the psalm are a prayer that Yahweh will
remember David's zeal in bringing the Ark to Jerusalem.

Lo we heard of it in Ephrathah, we found it in the fields of Jaar.
'Let us go to his dwelling place; let us worship at his footstool!'
Arise, O Lord, and go to thy resting place, thou and the Ark of thy
   might.
Let thy priests be clothed with righteousness, and let thy saints
   shout for joy.
For thy servant David's sake do not turn away the face of thy
   anointed one.

(vvs. 6–10)

The psalmist then introduces the people of David's time as
speakers, indicating how eagerly and joyfully they welcomed
David's proposal to bring the Ark to Jerusalem, and how they
resolved to worship Yahweh in his sanctuary there, praying for
blessing upon priests, people and King.

The Lord swore to David a sure oath from which he will not turn
   back:
'One of the sons of your body I will set on your throne.
If your sons keep my covenant and my testimonies which I shall
   teach them, their sons also for ever shall sit upon your throne.'
For the Lord has chosen Zion; he has desired it for his habitation:
'This is my resting place for ever; here will I dwell, for I have
   desired it.
I will abundantly bless her provisions; I will satisfy her poor with
   bread.
Her priests I will clothe with salvation, and her saints will shout
   for joy.

There I will make a horn to sprout for David; I have prepared a
lamp for my anointed.
His enemies I will clothe with shame, but upon himself his crown
will shed its lustre.'

(vvs. 11–18)

Yahweh now answers the prayers with which the psalm began.
He *will* remember David, for Jerusalem is his own chosen
place, and he *will* bless people and priests alike, and restore the
greatness of the House of David.

In giving a date to this psalm Kirkpatrick puts much emphasis
on the prayer that David should be 'remembered'. The implication here, he considers, is that David's work is seen as a far
off historical event. Hence the psalm probably had its historical
origin at a time when the nation of Israel had been restored to
Jerusalem following its exile in Babylon, and it is therefore,
'an encouragement to Israel of the Restoration to believe that
Jehovah will not fail to perform his promises to the House of
David. Those promises rested upon the choice of Zion as
Jehovah's earthly abode. The Restoration had proved that
Jehovah had not abandoned Jerusalem; it was a pledge that he
would not leave his promise to David unfulfilled. The re-
establishment of the worship which David founded in Jerusalem would be incomplete without the fulfilment of these
promises' (*The Psalms*, p. 763). Of the exact date in post-exilic
history to which the psalm should be ascribed, Kirkpatrick is
uncertain, but he tentatively assigns it to the age of the prophet
Nehemiah (*c.* 444 B.C.).

The striking contrast between this traditional interpretation
of *Psalm* 132 and its modern counterpart can be seen in detail in
Chapter Four.

Having illustrated something of the way followed by the
older commentators, it is now time to look at some of the basic
foundation principles of psalm study, on which there is general
agreement and from which contemporary views have been
developed.

Names of Psalms

The translators of the ancient Hebrew texts produced about
132 B.C. a Greek equivalent which is known as the 'Septuagint'
(often distinguished by the symbol LXX). The Greek word
used in the LXX to translate the Hebrew technical term for a
song with musical accompaniment, is *psalmos*. Hence the name
'psalm'. The Hebrew bible gives the title of the collection which
we know as psalms, a title which in Hebrew means 'Book of
Praises' or simply 'Praises', though it is interesting to note that
only one psalm in our collection, *Psalm* 145, carries the title 'A
song of praise'. Sometimes the Hebrew collection was known
by the title 'Prayers' – there are some five psalms which incor-
porate this title viz. *Pss.* 17; 86; 90; 102; 142.

Division of the Psalter

From quite early times, even before the LXX, the psalms have
been traditionally divided into five groups.

I – Psalms	1 – 41	III – Psalms	73 – 89
II – Psalms	42 – 72	IV – Psalms	90 – 106
	V – Psalms	107 – 150	

There is no specific evidence to suggest that there is any special
purpose for this division, but it is mentioned in both Jewish and
early Christian writings. In the Jewish exegetical material
known as the Midrash it is stated that Moses gave the Israelites
the five books of the Law, and to correspond to these David
gave them the book of psalms containing five books. Most of
the early Church Fathers also mention this division, offering
various reasons for its existence.

Individual titles of Psalms

These are not at all easy to sort out, as it would seem that many
of them are titles which have been added by later hands. There

are titles, for instance, which describe the character of the psalm, such as 'Song' or 'Praise' – these have already been mentioned above. Some titles relate to the musical setting or performance of the psalm, e.g. *Psalm* 4 – 'To the choirmaster, with stringed instruments'; *Psalm* 90 – 'A prayer of Moses the man of God'. Other psalms have titles which refer to their use liturgically, e.g. *Psalm* 92 – 'A song for the Sabbath'; *Psalm* 30 – 'A song at the dedication of the Temple'; *Psalm* 120 and others – 'A song of Ascents'. Then there are titles which purport to refer to authorship or origin – about seventy-three psalms bear the title 'Of David', whilst others are called after Moses (e.g. *Ps.* 90 above), Solomon (*Ps.* 72), and the Sons of Korah (*Ps.* 85). Lastly, there are titles which purport to refer to historical events in the reign of David, e.g. *Psalm* 51 – 'A psalm of David when Nathan the prophet came to him, after he had gone in to Bathsheba'.

There is general agreement that no reliability can be placed on these last two groups i.e. titles which refer either to authorship or historical circumstance, as it is frequently found impossible to reconcile the contents and language of the psalm in question with its title. Of the psalms which bear the name of David, for instance, there are many which assume circumstances and situations which do not in any way correspond with those of David's day, e.g. *Psalm* 69 'Save me O God' contains verses which read:

> I am the talk of those who sit in the gate, and the drunkards make songs about me.
>
> (v. 12)
>
> Insults have broken my heart, so that I am in despair.
> I looked for pity, but there was none; and for comforters, but I found none.
> They gave me poison for food, and for my thirst they gave me vinegar to drink.
>
> (vvs. 20–21)

Nor are the feelings expressed in some of these psalms easy to reconcile with those expected of a man of David's character. Again, in content, some psalms bearing David's name, are to be clearly dated at a much later stage of history and the evidence for this is to be found in the language and concepts employed. *Psalm* 139 is a good example in this respect, its whole tone reflecting a considered spirituality of a much later time than that of David :-

> O Lord thou hast searched me out and known me!
> Thou knowest when I sit down and when I rise up; thou discernest my thoughts from afar.
> Thou searchest out my path and my lying down, and art acquainted with all my ways.
> Even before a word is on my tongue, lo, O Lord, thou knowest it altogether.
> Thou dost beset me behind and before, and layest thy hand upon me.
> Such knowledge is too wonderful for me; it is high, I cannot attain it.
> Whither shall I go from thy Spirit? Or whither shall I flee from thy presence?
> If I ascend to heaven, thou art there! If I make my bed in Sheol, thou art there!
> If I take the wings of the morning and dwell in the uttermost parts of the sea, even there thy hand shall lead me, and thy right hand shall hold me.
> If I say, 'Let only darkness cover me, and the light about me be night',
> Even the darkness is not dark to thee, the night is bright as the day; for darkness is as light with thee.
>
> (vvs. 1–12)

So it is accepted that the value of the psalm titles as they stand in the Old Testament book lies in the fact that they give a general indication of the *source* from which they were derived, rather than a clue to actual authorship. Thus 'The Psalms of the Sons of Korah' is probably part of the title of a group of psalms written by members of the family of Korah, and preserved in a special collection. The same is likely to be the case with those psalms which are entitled 'Psalms of Asaph', and of course also of the 'Psalms of David'.

Yet one word of caution is needed here. The reader may consider from the arguments adduced above, that it is only the content of a psalm which gives a truly reliable guide to its historical place in the history of Israel. This assumption itself is questionable, as the fact that a psalm may have been altered by a later writer or writers must always be taken into account. Careful examination of certain psalms clearly shows that a later editor has sometimes altered, divided, or revised sections of a psalm for some special purpose of his own. An example here is *Psalm* 18 which can be compared with the original historical narrative in *2 Sam.* 22. The Psalm reads:

> I love thee, O Lord, my strength.
> The Lord is my rock, and my fortress, and my deliverer, my God, my rock, in whom I take my refuge, my shield, and the horn of my salvation, my stronghold.
> I call upon the Lord, who is worthy to be praised, and I am saved from my enemies.
> The cords of death encompassed me, the torrents of perdition assailed me; the cords of Sheol entangled me, the snares of death confronted me.
>
> (vvs. 1–5)

The historical narrative in *2 Sam.* reads: 'He (i.e. David) said,

> The Lord is my rock, and my fortress, and my deliverer, my God, my rock, in whom I take refuge, my shield and the horn of salvation, my stronghold and my refuge, my saviour; thou savest me from violence.
> I call upon the Lord, who is worthy to be praised, and I am saved from my enemies.
> For the waves of death encompassed me, the torrents of perdition assailed me; the cords of Sheol entangled me, the snares of death confronted me.
>
> (vvs. 2–6)

The differences are slight – but they are differences!

Age of the Psalms

All things considered then, it is possible, as a result of careful examination of the thought forms and content of the psalms, to arrive at a general conclusion regarding their place in Israel's history. In this respect it is of particular note that at the turn of the century commentators should have been defending the date of certain psalms as being pre-exilic (i.e. before 597 B.C. when the first of the people of Jerusalem were carried away captive to Babylon), against strenuous attacks from more radical quarters. The great biblical scholar Wellhausen, wrote, 'Since the Psalter belongs to the Hagiographa, and is the hymn book of the congregation of the Second Temple . . . the question is not whether it contains any post-exilic Psalms, but whether it contains any pre-exilic Psalms'. And again, Professor Cheyne in his Bampton Lectures for 1889 maintained that the whole Psalter, with the possible exception of *Psalm* 18 was post-exilic, belonging to the later Persian and Greek period, and containing a large number of Maccabean psalms edited finally by Simon the Maccabee in about 140 B.C.! Another scholar, Duhm (1900), adopted an even more radical view, and not only denied the existence in the Psalter of a single psalm that could be designated pre-exilic, but expressed considerable doubt that *any* psalm could be dated as early even as the Persian period (i.e. before *c.* 540 B.C.). Against views such as these writers like Kirkpatrick soundly defended pre-exilic dating on ground of content, and association with historical events which took place before the exile.

Object, collection and growth of the Psalter

One of the titles of the Psalter frequently used by older writers is 'Hymnbook of the Second Temple'. But whilst there is undoubtedly in it a great deal of material which can be regarded as being suitable for liturgical use, there is also much which could hardly have been written for this particular purpose. The general intention of the compilers was probably to make a collection of the religious poetry which did in fact exist – hence there are psalms which are suitable not only for liturgical use, but also for public and private devotions. If the internal evidence of the psalter is carefully examined, it seems reasonably certain that the book is an omnibus collection of various smaller collections which had independent historical, liturgical and personal subjects. Thus, Kirkpatrick (*op. cit.* p. lviii) constructs a neat table of suggested 'steps in the formation of the Psalter' moving from an original collection bearing the title 'Psalms of David', to the complete edition as it is in our Bible, and ranging in date from the period of the Monarchy (i.e. forward from *c.* 1025 B.C.) down to about 200 B.C. He concludes that although the opinion of his day was that the Psalter in all its parts was a compilation of the post-exilic age, nevertheless this does not exclude the possibility that pre-exilic collections of psalms existed, side by side with prophetic and historical books.

These then are some of the foundation principles of traditional psalm interpretation which were accepted at the turn of the century. But exciting new ideas were already beginning to come to the fore, even as Kirkpatrick's commentary was published in 1902, and soon there were set in motion new insights and theories which were to revolutionize this field of biblical study. The impetus was given in the outstanding work of one man, Hermann Gunkel. The essence of Gunkel's approach to the psalms lay in the fact that he believed that in the ancient world, the power of custom was greater than it is today, and that a real understanding of ancient literature can only be properly understood by examining its forms and also the real-life situation which brought it into being. He further considered it of immense value to compare national forms and situations with those of neighbouring countries and cultures. From comparative studies of this kind, Gunkel was able to classify the psalms into five principal groups or 'types', all of them having their origin in the early religious observance of Israel.

1. The Hymn. This was originally intended to be sung by either individual or choir, as a part of the normal Temple worship. In later times the hymn probably became a free composition of its author's own personal adoration or devotion, unrelated to set Temple Liturgies. An example is *Psalm* 8:

> O Lord, our Lord, how majestic is thy name in all the earth!
> Thou whose glory above the heavens is chanted by the mouths of babes and infants, thou hast founded a bulwark because of thy foes, to still the enemy and the avenger.
> When I look at thy heavens, the work of thy fingers, the moon and the stars which thou hast established; what is man that thou art mindful of him, and the son of man that thou dost care for him? Yet thou hast made him little less than God, and dost crown him with glory and honour.
> Thou hast given him dominion over the works of thy hands; thou hast put all things under his feet, all sheep and oxen, and also the beasts of the field, the birds of the air, and the fish of the sea, whatever passes along the paths of the sea.
> O Lord, our Lord, how majestic is thy name in all the earth!

A biblical reference to this kind of public hymn, is *Amos* 5:23 'Take away from me the noise of your songs; to the melody of your harps I will not listen'.

Other psalms in this group are *Pss.* 8; 19; 29; 33; 65; 68; 96; 98; 100; 103; 104; 105; 111; 114; 115; 117; 135; 136; 145; 147; 148; 149; 150.

2. Communal laments. As the name suggests, these psalms spring from the experience of some general calamity which threatened the whole of society, e.g. famine or invasion by a foreign army. They were probably sung at a general assembly in the sanctuary, and accompanied by displays of public grief such as wailing or beating the breast. *Psalm* 80 is typical of this group of laments:

> Give ear, O shepherd of Israel, thou who leadest Joseph like a flock!

Thou who art enthroned upon the cherubim, shine forth before
    Ephraim and Benjamin and Manasseh!

Stir up thy might, and come to save us!

Restore us, O God; let thy face shine, that we may be saved!

O Lord God of Hosts, how long wilt thou be angry with thy
    people's prayers?

Thou hast fed them with the bread of tears, and given them tears to
    drink in full measure.

Thou dost make us the scorn of our neighbours; and our enemies
    laugh among themselves.

Restore us, O God of Hosts; let thy face shine, that we may be
    saved!

Thou didst bring a vine out of Egypt; thou didst drive out the
    nations and plant it.

Thou didst clear the ground for it; it took deep root and filled the
    land.

The mountains were covered with its shade, the mighty cedars
    with its branches; it sent out its branches to the sea and its
    shoots to the River.

Why then hast thou broken down its walls, so that all who pass
    along the way pluck its fruit?

The boar from the forest ravages it, and all that move in the field
    feed on it.

Turn again, O God of Hosts!

Look down from heaven, and see; have regard for this vine, the
    stock which thy right hand planted.

They have burned it with fire, they have cut it down; may they
    perish at the rebuke of thy countenance!

But let thy hand be upon the man of thy right hand, the son of
    man whom thou hast made strong for thyself!

Then we will never turn back from thee; give us life, and we will
    call upon thy name!

Restore us, O Lord God of Hosts! let thy face shine, that we may
    be saved!

In the biblical narrative, *Judges* 20: 26 ff. clearly indicates a
situation of this kind:

'Then all the people of Israel, the whole army, went up and

came to Bethel and wept; they sat before the Lord, and fasted that day until evening, and offered burnt offerings and peace offerings before the Lord. And the people of Israel enquired of the Lord (for the Ark of the covenant of God was there in those days, and Phineas the son of Elizar, son of Aaron, ministered before it in those days), saying, "Shall we yet again go out to battle against our brethren the Benjaminites, or shall we cease?". And the Lord said, "Go up; for tomorrow I will give them into your hand".'

Other laments of a similar kind are *Pss.* 44; 74; 79; 80; 83; and to a certain extent *Pss.* 58; 106 and 125.

3. Royal Psalms. In all of these, the principal figure is one that can only be explained as a native Israelite king. Old Testament literature of the period certainly shows that the king was regarded as having a specially intimate relationship with Yahweh, and that he played a most important part in public worship. An example of such participation is to be found in *1 Sam.* 26: 11 where it is suggested that, having been ceremonially anointed with the title of Messiah of Yahweh, the king is therefore sacred and inviolable. Thus David, who comes upon King Saul whilst he is resting in a cave, and who might well have put him to death there and then, says: 'The Lord forbid that I should put forth my hand against the Lord's anointed; but take now the spear that is at his head, and the jar of water, and let us go.'

Then too, after his own coronation, David plays a leading part in the ceremony which accompanied the bringing of the Ark to Jerusalem. *2 Sam.* 6: 14, a familiar text, reads: 'And David danced before the Lord with all his might; and David was girded with a linen ephod. So David and all the house of Israel brought up the Ark of the Lord with shouting, and with the sound of the horn.' That the sanctuaries at both Jerusalem and Bethel were originally royal sanctuaries is almost certain. *1 Kings* 5: 15 ff. gives a detailed account of Solomon's personal involvement in the building of the first temple at Jerusalem, and the Prophet Amos is told by Amaziah (*Amos* 7. 12 f.): 'O seer, go, flee flee away to the land of Judah, and eat bread and prophesy there; but never again prophesy at Bethel, for it is the king's sanctuary, and it is a temple of the kingdom.' There are further examples in the temple ritual where the king either offers sacrifice or has it offered on his behalf. Solomon, for example, '. . . went to Gibeon to sacrifice there, for that was the great high place; Solomon used to offer a thousand burnt offerings upon the altar' (*1 Kings*. 3. 4). And there are many occasions when we find mention of public intercession being made by the king before he goes into battle. Thus, when the Moabites and Ammonites come to fight against Jehoshaphat, who reigned over the Kingdom of Judah in the middle of the ninth century B.C., 'Then Jehoshaphat feared, and set himself to seek the Lord, and proclaimed a fast throughout all Judah. And Judah assembled to seek help from the Lord; from all the cities of Judah they came to seek the Lord. And Jehoshaphat stood in the assembly of Judah and Jerusalem, in the house of the Lord before the new court, and said, "O Lord, God of our fathers, art thou not God in heaven? Dost thou not rule over all the kingdoms of the nations? . . . Now behold the men of Ammon and Moab and Mount Seir. . . . O our God, wilt thou not execute judgement upon them? For we are powerless against this great multitude that is coming against us. We do not know what to do, but our eyes are upon thee".' (*2 Chron*. 20: 3–6; 12).

In the light of this kind of evidence, therefore, Gunkel assigned his royal psalms to specific occasions in the life of the king:

(*a*) The anniversary of the founding of the Davidic dynasty and the royal sanctuary. *Psalm* 132 (see page 11 f.).

(*b*) The enthronement of the king. *Psalm* 2 (look also at *Pss.* 101; 110):

Why do the nations conspire, and the peoples plot in vain? The
kings of the earth set themselves, and the rulers take counsel to-
gether, against the Lord and against his anointed, saying,
'Let us burst their bonds asunder, and cast their cords from us.'
He who sits in the heavens laughs; the Lord has them in derision.
Then he will speak to them in his wrath, and terrify them in his
        fury, saying,
'I have set my king on Zion, my holy hill.'

(vvs. 1–6)

(c) The anniversary of the king's birthday or his wedding.
Psalm 21 (look also at *Pss.* 45; 52):

In thy strength the king rejoices, O Lord; and in thy help how
        greatly he exults!
Thou hast given him his heart's desire, and hast not withheld the
        request of his lips.
For thou dost meet him with goodly blessings; thou dost set a
        crown of fine gold upon his head.
He asked life of thee; thou gavest it to him, length of days for ever
        and ever.
His glory is great through thy help; splendour and majesty thou
        dost bestow upon him.
Yes, thou dost make him most blessed for ever; thou dost make
        him glad with the joy of thy presence.
For the king trusts in the Lord; and through the steadfast love of
        the Most High he shall not be moved.

(vvs. 1–7)

(d) Prayers to God before going out into battle. *Psalm* 20:
(look also at *Ps.* 144: 1–11):

The Lord answer you in the day of trouble! The name of the God
        of Jacob protect you!
May he send you help from the sanctuary, and give you support
        from Zion!
May he remember all your offerings, and regard with favour your
        burnt sacrifices!
May he grant you your heart's desire, and fulfil all your plans!

May we shout for joy over your victory, and in the name of
our God set up our banners! May the Lord fulfil all your
petitions!

Now I know that the Lord will help his anointed; he will answer
him from his holy heaven with mighty victories by his right hand.

Some boast of chariots, and some of horses; but we boast of the
name of the Lord our God.

They will collapse and fall; but we will rise and stand upright.

Give victory to the king, O Lord; answer us when we call.

(*e*) Occasions of thanksgiving after a triumphal return from
battle. *Psalm* 18:

Thou didst deliver me from strife with the peoples; thou didst
make me the head of the nations; people whom I had not known
served me.

As soon as they heard of me they obeyed me; foreigners came
cringing to me.

Foreigners lost heart, and came trembling out of their fastnesses.

The Lord lives; and blessed be my rock, and exalted be the God
of my salvation, the God who gave me vengeance and subdued
peoples under me; who delivered me from my enemies; yea, thou
didst exalt me above my adversaries; thou didst deliver me from
men of violence.

For this I will extol thee, O Lord, among the nations, and sing
praises to thy name.

Great triumphs he gives to his king, and shows steadfast love to
his anointed, to David and his descendants for ever.

(vvs. 43–50)

4. Individual laments. These psalms Gunkel noted, had a
common theme – the worshipper is in some form of deep dis-
tress, and he laments with great intensity that he is constantly
persecuted or slandered by an enemy. Typical of a large number
of such psalms is *Psalm* 3:

O Lord, how many are my foes! Many are rising against me;
many are saying of me, there is no help for him in God.

But thou, O Lord, art a shield about me,
my glory, and the lifter of my head.

I cry aloud to the Lord, and he answers me from his holy hill.
I lie down and sleep; I wake again, for the Lord sustains me.
I am not afraid of ten thousands of people who have set themselves
    against me round about.
Arise, O Lord! Deliver me, O my God! For thou dost smite all
    my enemies on the cheek, thou dost break the teeth of the
    wicked.
Deliverance belongs to the Lord! thy blessing be upon thy people!

A great number of similar individual laments include *Psalms*
5; 6; 7; 13; 17; 22; 25; 26; 27. 7–14; 28; 31; 35; 38; 39; 42; 43;
51; 54; 55; 56; 57; 59; 61; 63; 64; 69; 70; 71; 86; 88; 102; 109;
120; 130; 140; 141; 142; 143.

5. Individual songs of thanksgiving. There are comparatively few
of these (*Pss.* 18; 32; 34; 41; 66; 92; 96; 118; 138). *Psalm* 30
serves as a good example:

I will extol thee, O Lord, for thou hast drawn me up, and hast not
    let my foes rejoice over me.
O Lord my God, I cried to thee for help, and thou hast healed me.
O Lord, thou hast brought up my soul from Sheol, restored me to
    life from among those gone down to the pit . . .
To thee, O Lord, I cried; and to the Lord I made supplication:
'What profit is there in my death, if I go down to the pit?
Will the dust praise thee? Will it tell of thy faithfulness?
Hear, O Lord, and be gracious to me! O Lord, be thou my helper!'
Thou hast turned for me my mourning into dancing; thou hast
    loosed my sackcloth and girded me with gladness, that my soul
    may praise thee and not be silent.
O Lord my God, I will give thanks to thee for ever.

(vvs. 1–3; 8–12)

Finally, Gunkel defines a series of smaller categories which
have titles which are self-explanatory. These are 'Songs of
Pilgrimage' – e.g. *Psalm* 84: 'How lovely is thy dwelling-
place'; Communal songs of thanksgiving – e.g. *Psalm* 67:
'May God be gracious to us and bless us'; 'Wisdom poetry'–
e.g. *Psalm* 127: 'Unless the Lord builds the house'; 'Liturgy'
– e.g. *Psalm* 24: 'The earth is the Lord's' and a group

of psalms which cannot be absolutely classified, called 'Mixed poems' – e.g. *Psalm* 40: 'I waited patiently for the Lord'.

Gunkel's insight in relating the content of the psalms not only to their history but to the religious observance of Israel which is known to us through that same history, opened up a completely new prospect for Old Testament study. Few writers since his day have failed to show the influence of his work. But there is another great name in modern psalm study, the name of a man who was to build upon the foundations laid by Gunkel, a theory of psalm interpretation which has completely changed the outlook of students of the psalms – that name is Sigmund Mowinckel.

Mowinckel openly acknowledged that his own work was based upon that of Gunkel, and that it was to the latter that he owed his enthusiasm for the subject. *All* the psalms were, for him, deeply embedded in the religious observance of Israel, a part of Israel's cultic history. His really great contribution to the field however was his contention that in ancient Israel there was an annual New Year Festival, observed in the temple in the autumn, at which Yahweh's enthronement as universal king was both celebrated and dramatically portrayed. The basis for his theory were *Psalms* 47; 93; 95–100, most of which begin with the same two Hebrew words which Mowinckel interpreted to read 'Yahweh has become king'. This expression, he considered, was to be understood in the light of the cultic observances in the countries round about Israel, notably in Babylon where the New Year Festival was celebrated with the Babylonian God Marduk in the leading role. In developing his theory, Mowinckel extended Gunkel's group of royal psalms so that the complete list included *Psalms* 2; 18; 20; 21; 28; 44; 45; 60: 61; 63; 66; 68; 72; 80; 83; 84; 89; 101; 110; 118; 132; 144 and also *1 Samuel* 2: 1–10 and *2 Samuel* 23: 1–7.

As Mowinckel's theory forms the real core of the psalm interpretation with which this volume is concerned, an outline of what he considered the New Year Festival to have been like would not at this stage be amiss.

Primarily, the festival was one of renewal, that is, on this occasion, year by year, Yahweh repeated his original triumph over primeval chaos (i.e. as recorded in *Genesis* 1) and his work in creation. This ceremony took the form of a ritual drama, with Yahweh triumphing over the kings and nations of the earth who represented chaos, and with the Ark, the symbol of his presence, being carried in procession to the sanctuary where he was freshly acclaimed as the universal king. In this ceremony the faith of Yahweh's chosen people is shown to be vindicated and the covenant with them and the house of David is renewed (the latter is represented by the reigning king). Israel is thus assured of good fortune for the coming year. It is noteworthy that Mowinckel gives the festival a place in the early history of Israel. He considers, for instance, that Isaiah's vision and call (*Isaiah* 6) took place on such a festival day and that the festival itself might have had its roots in the pre-Davidic worship of El Elyon, mention of which can be found in *Genesis* 14: 18 ff.

With this brief outline, and with the realization of its crucial importance to the basic theories of contemporary psalm interpretation in mind, it is now time to turn to a detailed look at the ancient New Year Festival of the people of Israel.

CHAPTER TWO

The New Year Festival

THE PRECEDING CHAPTER HAS INDICATED SOMETHING of the tremendous importance which is attached to the New Year Festival in contemporary treatment of the Psalms. It is understandable too, if readers familiar with their Bibles are now racking their brains in an effort to call to mind such a festival as that outlined in Chapter One. The truth of the matter is that there is no exact description at all in the Old Testament, but despite this fact we are able to accept with confidence statements such as that of S. H. Hooke (*Peake's Commentary*, p. 146, para. 116c), who assures us that 'the existence of such a festival and the central part played therein by the King as an essential element in the pattern of Israelite religion under the monarchy is now generally accepted'. Readers who wish to examine further the grounds for this statement are referred in particular to the work of Mowinckel and A. R. Johnson (*Psalmenstudien ii* and *Sacral Kingship in Ancient Israel* respectively).

Now what evidence can in fact be adduced from the Bible itself for the existence of the New Year Festival? Who organized it and who attended it? At which period of Israelite history was it begun and for how long did it continue? Finally, what is believed to have been the general pattern of the festival? All these are questions which demand an answer if a convincing case is to be made out for interpreting and understanding the Psalms in the way which was outlined in Chapter One. We can find answers to them which will allow, or even encourage this interpretation; though it would be wise to bear in mind that they are not accepted by scholars as amounting to positive proof.[1]

We must at once admit that the marshalling of evidence in this connection is no easy task, for the Old Testament, whilst containing many references to the religious festivals and observances of Ancient Israel, does not present us with anything like a clear and orderly scheme either as regards the time at which they were celebrated or their ceremonial. Also, as much of the Old Testament was written down long after the actual events described and sometimes revised and altered by successive editors, it cannot therefore be used as a primary source of information. Indeed it may be considered a fair criticism of the authors of some of the more extreme views on the Festival, that they have failed to heed the warning of the German theologian Martin Noth who wrote, 'We can obtain . . . an approximate picture of what Israel considered essential in the celebrations held at the solemn gatherings of the tribes, but we must be careful not to attempt to reconstruct the whole situation from the scanty and purely indirect information in the Old Testament' (*History of Israel*, p. 100). Of course there is a definite place for intelligent conjecture, and having made this point we can now go on to explore the biblical foundation upon which the New Year Festival theories are based.

For a long time, both during and following the Conquest of Canaan, the Israelites worshipped Yahweh at local shrines which were scattered throughout the land. The Canaanites were essentially an agricultural people, and as a result their worship was centred on the process of nature and the annual cycle of the seasons. In fact it was an agricultural religion, the

[1] See for example, Professor G. W. Anderson *op. cit.* p. 411 para. 36ob – 'This theory has been and still is criticised as being based on misleading analogies from other religions; and there are still those who would interpret the Enthronement pss. in terms of history or of eschatology.'

whole aim of which was '. . . to secure the hearty co-operation of the deity in the production of the various crops' (Oesterley and Robinson, *Hebrew Religion*, p. 180). Once the Israelites were settled in the land it is not surprising to find them taking over Canaanite forms of worship as well as a belief in the Ba'als, the local Canaanite gods who were held to be the divine owners of the soil. It is this turning away from the true worship of Yahweh that the writer of the Book of Judges sees as a direct cause of the various ills which befell the Israelites at this period in their history (*c.* 1200 B.C. onwards). There is a recurrent formula which reads, 'And the people of Israel did what was evil in the sight of the Lord, forgetting the Lord their God, and serving the Ba'als and the Ashe'roth. Therefore the anger of the Lord was kindled against Israel and he sold them into the hand of . . .' (*Judges* 2 : 11 ff., for example).

It is generally assumed that the festivals and accompanying sacrifices of Canaanite religion at this period were similar to those observed in other parts of the ancient East. The principal festivals were three in number – one that took place in the autumn, at the end of one year and at the beginning of the next; the spring festival which marked the beginning of the harvest; and the festival which came some seven or so weeks after and which marked the end of the wheat harvest. Sacrifice was no new thing to the Israelites (G. W. Anderson, *op. cit.* p. 162, para 131c – 'There can be little doubt that sacrifice, at least in simple forms, belonged to Mosaic religion . . .'). Agricultural festivals certainly were something new, and in the same way as the early Christian Church took over pagan festivals and used them, but with a completely different content and outlook, the Israelites took over existing Canaanite festivals and gradually converted them from festivals honouring the Ba'als to festivals honouring Yahweh and at the same time linked with great events in Israelite history.

So then, by the time the Israelite tribes were well-established in Canaan the principal festivals were:

The Passover Feast (main reference *Deut.* 16: 1-8). This feast was celebrated March to April and was originally linked with the Canaanite feast of Unleavened Bread (see p. 31). There were three definite parts to it – first, an animal was sacrificed: 'And you shall offer the Passover sacrifice to the Lord your God from the flock or the herd . . .' (*Deut.* 16: 2). It seems that this animal was to be a firstling – 'Your lamb shall be without blemish, a male a year old . . .' (*Exod.* 12: 5). Next the sacrificial victim was offered then eaten during the night – '. . . nor shall any of the flesh which you sacrifice on the evening of the first day remain all night until morning' (*Deut.* 16: 4). Finally the blood of the victim was smeared on the outside of the dwelling-places of the worshippers – 'Then shall they take some of the blood, and put it on the two doorposts and the lintel of the houses in which they eat them (i.e. the sacrificial lambs)' (*Exod.* 12: 7). The great event in Israelite history with which this festival was linked was of course the Exodus from Egypt (see *Exod.* 12: 17 – 'And you shall observe the feast of unleavened bread, for on this very day I brought your hosts out of the land of Egypt: therefore you shall observe this day, throughout your generations as an ordinance for ever').

The Feast of Weeks, or harvest, or first-fruits (main reference *Deut.* 16: 9-12). This feast was celebrated seven weeks after the Passover Feast on the fiftieth day and it marked the wheat harvest. The occasion was one of general rejoicing and an offering to Yahweh of the first-fruits of the wheat – 'Then you shall keep the feast of weeks to the Lord your God with the tribute of a freewill offering . . . and you shall rejoice before the Lord your God . . .' (*Deut.* 16: 10-11). It was linked in later Judaism with the giving of the Law to Moses at Horeb, but as this connection was made in the Maccabean period (*c.* 170 B.C. onwards), there is no reference to it in the Canonical books of the Old Testament.

The Feast of Tabernacles or Ingathering (main reference *Deut.*

16: 13–15; cf. *Lev.* 23: 33 ff.). This feast was celebrated in the autumn; September to October, which was the end of the old economic year. That it was an occasion of considerable importance may be drawn from the fact that amongst the many references to it in the Old Testament (e.g. *Jud.* 21: 19; *1 Kings* 8: 2; 12: 32; *Ezek.* 45: 25; and others), there are striking references which simply call it 'the Feast' without any further elaboration (e.g. *1 Kings* 8: 2; 12: 32).

Information about the festival includes the familiar practice of dwelling in 'tents' or 'booths' (see *Lev.* 23: 40 ff. – 'And you shall take on the first day the fruit of goodly trees, branches of palm trees . . . You shall dwell in booths for seven days . . .'), and considerable detail regarding the daily sacrifices (see *Num.* 29: 12–38 – 'On the fifteenth day of the seventh month you shall have a holy convocation . . . and you shall offer a burnt offering . . . thirteen young bulls, two rams, fourteen male lambs a year old . . . and their cereal offering of fine flour . . . also one male goat for a sin offering . . .' Similar instructions follow for each day of the feast). On the eighth day of the feast there is to be a solemn assembly (*Num.* 29: 35). Finally a very important verse in the post-exilic book of Zechariah gives us some indirect evidence which helps in the reconstruction of the ritual of the festival – 'Then every one that survives of all the nations that have come against Jerusalem shall go up year after year to worship the King, the Lord of hosts and to keep the feast of booths. And if any of the families of the earth do not go up to Jerusalem to worship the King, the Lord of hosts, there will be no rain upon them' (*Zech.* 14: 16 ff.). The connection of the gift of rain and worship of Yahweh as King mentioned here, with the celebration of the Feast of Tabernacles, will be made clear in a later chapter when the liturgical significance of the Psalms themselves is considered in relation to the ritual of the Feast. It is only necessary to add that later Judaism associated the Feast with the 'booths' or 'tents' of the wanderings in the

wilderness following the Exodus from Egypt (see *Lev.* 23 : 42 ff. –
'You shall dwell in booths ... that your generations may know
that I made the people of Israel dwell in booths when I brought
them out of the land of Egypt ...').

This tripartite pattern of festivals is repeated in numerous
Old Testament books (cf. *Exod.* 12 f.; 23: 14–17; *Lev.* 23;
Num. 28 f. and others). It is the Feast of Tabernacles, or Booths
which is of particular interest to us in this study, for it is this
festival which is in fact taken to be the Autumn or New Year
Festival which we are considering.

So much then for representative biblical evidence for the
Festival. We turn now to try and discover who organized it and
who formed the congregation attending it. From earliest times
in the history of Israel there appear to have been priests – indeed
the setting aside of certain persons to perform priestly functions
is a feature common to all forms of religion. There are differing strands of tradition in the Old Testament concerning the
origin of Yahweh's priests, but the generally accepted view of
Old Testament writers is that the priesthood was the special
concern of the family of Moses. The later Jerusalem priesthood
traced its descent from Moses' brother Aaron (*Exod.* 40: 12 ff.).
Another tradition considers the priesthood to have originated
from Joshua (*Exod.* 33: 11). A theory of the institution of
priesthood which is related to our present study and which is in
itself quite fascinating, is that of A. R. Johnson. In his book
Sacral Kingship in Ancient Israel (p. 41 ff.), he outlines a theory
which suggests the amalgamation of the Mosaic priesthood
with those priests who were found in Jebus (later Jerusalem)
after its capture by David. These priests were leaders of the
worship of 'God Most High' in Jebus and were descended from
the royal priestly order of Melchizedek. It was Abram who
showed great deference towards Melchizedek, King of Salem
(identified in Johnson's theory with Jerusalem. Cf. for example
Psalm 110: 4: 'The Lord has sworn and will not change his
mind, You are a priest for ever after the order of Melchizedek.'

The association of Melchizedek here with Zion in verse 2 and the fact that this psalm is being sung in the temple at Jerusalem are sufficient evidence to make the identification). The text of this historic meeting reads, 'After his (i.e. Abram's) return from the defeat of Chedorlaomer and the kings who were with him, the king of Sodom went out to meet him in the Valley of Shaveh (that is, the King's Valley). And Melchizedek king of Salem brought out bread and wine; he was a priest of God Most High. And he blessed him and said, "Blessed be Abram by God Most High, maker of heaven and earth; and blessed be God Most High, who has delivered your enemies into your hand!" And Abram gave him a tenth of everything' (*Gen.* 14: 17–20). Thus, having captured the city of Jebus, '. . . David found in the Jebusite cultus with its worship of the "Most High" and its royal priestly order of Melchizedek a ritual and mythology which might prove to be the means of carrying out Yahweh's purposes for Israel and fusing the chosen people into a model of national righteousness' (*op. cit.*, p. 46).

It seems then, that there was an organized priesthood ministering at the central shrine in Jerusalem as well as at local shrines throughout the land, and that these priests were the descendants of priests who had performed similar functions in earlier days of Israel's history. The centralization of worship at Jerusalem after its capture by David led to a much more highly organized system of priestly functions there (e.g. the organization of the priesthood into 'courses', see *1 Chron.* 24: 7 ff. Cf. *Luke* 1: 8 – Zechariah is ministering in the temple 'when his division was on duty, according to the custom of the priesthood. . .'; also the establishment of temple musicians and singers, see *2 Sam.* 6: 5 – 'And David and all the house of Israel were making merry before the Lord with all their might, with songs and lyres and harps and tambourines and castanets and cymbals'). It would be these priests, singers and musicians who would have been responsible for the organization and performance of the ritual and liturgy of the New Year Festival itself.

As to the identity of the worshippers at this and other annual festivals, we are left in no doubt – 'Three times a year all your males shall appear before the Lord your God at the place which he will choose . . .' (*Deut.* 16: 16).

Now what can be said about the date in Israelite history when the festival became established? In this connection it is not easy to be exact. The Deuteronomic writer places the festival as being a part of Yahweh's instructions to Israel via Moses (*Deut.* 16), but this is an example of post-exilic 'editing' of history and cannot be taken to represent the true facts; a festival of the kind we are considering would only have developed in a settled and stable community, that is an environment vastly different from that of the wanderings in the wilderness. However it is suggested that David's establishment of the Ark in Jerusalem (*2 Sam.* 6) may well have been the inauguration of the New Year Festival in itself. It is also possible that this event was in fact the adaptation by Israel of a feast long observed in the city (formerly Jebus, see above) prior to its capture by David. Certainly the worship which marked the dedication of Solomon's temple is clearly that of the New Year Festival (see *1 Kings* 8: 2 – 'And all the men of Israel assembled to King Solomon at the feast in the month Ethanim, which is the seventh month.' Cf. *2 Chron.* 5: 3; 7: 8–9).

The end of the monarchy and the final destruction of the temple at Jerusalem (586 B.C.) not only brought to an end temple worship, but also marked the end of the particular relationship which had existed between the King and this worship. This relationship is not explicitly described in the Bible, since our texts were revised after the Babylonian exile. However, when eventually the exiles returned to Jerusalem and the temple began to function once more, it was clear that many important changes had taken place.

There remains our final question – what form did the New Year Festival take? The Old Testament references which have been quoted so far, give us details of the sacrifices which were

to be offered to Yahweh – what they were, the number of
them and the exact kind of sacrifice which was to be offered
on particular days (see pp. 32 ff. above). At the end of the
feast there was a solemn assembly (*Num.* 29: 35 – 'On the
eighth day you shall have a solemn assembly . . .') – what were
the ritual events which marked the climax of the festival and
this solemn assembly? Before attempting to answer this question it is worth stating once again that the details of the New
Year Festival which follow are not to be found in this form in
the Old Testament. The reconstruction of events is based on
activities which scholars know took place in the worship of
surrounding nations at this period in history, and on an assumption, now widely accepted, that '. . . we have to look upon
Israelite Canaan as part of a vast culture area of the Near East,
dominated by Babylonian culture patterns, and this not only in
the field of religion, but in spiritual and material culture in
general' (G. Widengren, Essay in *Myth, Ritual & Kingship*, ed.
S. H. Hooke, p. 156).

Inside and outside the Temple in Jerusalem then, on this
great festival day, was enacted a splendid, dramatic pageant,
accompanied by songs and music, which followed a pattern
something like this:

(*a*) <u>Yahweh, as leader of the forces of light, triumphs over the</u>
<u>powers of darkness which are represented by the chaotic waters</u>
<u>of the primeval ocean.</u> It is possible that this triumph was acted
symbolically with the bronze 'sea' which stood outside the
Temple featuring in the ritual drama. The bronze 'sea' was a
great bowl of over 16,000 gallons capacity, and it is probable
that in itself it represented the 'great deep' and consequently the
primeval struggle between Yahweh and Tehom (the ancient
name for the 'deep' or 'ocean'). The placing of the bronze 'sea'
outside the Temple is recorded in *1 Kings* 7: 23 ff. – 'Then he
(Solomon) made the molten sea; it was round, ten cubits from
brim to brim . . . it held two thousand baths.' It is possible
that 'waves' were simulated in this 'sea' by members of the

congregation, and that at a certain point when these were at their roughest, the Davidic King who represented Yahweh, either by word or gesture caused the water to return to a state of calmness. It is also possible that this part of the cult ritual may have taken the form of a cult lyric sung perhaps by the Temple choirs, with the congregation standing round the bronze 'sea'. Alternatively, and perhaps most likely, this part of the drama might have included both the symbolic ritual *and* the cult lyrics. At any rate, Yahweh is acclaimed victor over the chaotic waters and is hailed as a mighty king, enthroned in the assembly of the gods. A cult-lyric which might have been used here either by itself or as an accompaniment to the symbolic 'stilling' of the 'sea' is *Psalm* 89, vv. 5–10:

> Let the heavens praise thy wonders, O Lord, thy faithfulness in the assembly of the Holy Ones!
> For who in the skies can be compared to the Lord? Who among the heavenly beings is like the Lord,
> A God feared in the council of the holy ones, great and terrible above all that are round about him?
> O Lord God of hosts, who is mighty as thou art, O Lord, with thy faithfulness round about thee?
> Thou dost rule the raging of the sea; when its waves rise thou stillest them.
> Thou didst crush Rahab like a carcass, thou didst scatter thy enemies with thy mighty arm.

In this initial stage of the festival, Yahweh's power and might are further extolled; they are revealed in his creation of the world and in historic events. *Psalm* 95 (The 'Venite') could have been sung as a cult-lyric to illustrate this:

> O come, let us sing to the Lord; let us make a joyful noise to the rock of our salvation!
> Let us come into his presence with thanksgiving; let us make a joyful noise to him with songs of praise!
> For the Lord is a great God, and a great King above all gods.

In his hand are the depths of the earth; the heights of the mountains are his also.

The sea is his, for he made it; for his hands formed the dry land.

O come, let us worship and bow down, let us kneel before the Lord, our Maker!

For he is our God, and we are the people of his pasture, and the sheep of his hand.

O that today you would hearken to his voice! Harden not your hearts, as at Meribah, as on the day at Massah in the wilderness.

when your fathers tested me, and put me to the proof, though they had seen my work.

For forty years I loathed that generation and said, 'They are a people who err in heart, and they do not regard my ways.'

Therefore I swore in my anger that they should not enter my rest.

(*b*) The great 'Day of Yahweh' is presented dramatically, that is the day when Yahweh, supreme source of light and life, will finally triumph over all the rebellious Gods and earthly nations who represent darkness and death. This part of the ritual would be observed outside the Temple, and would almost certainly consist of a mimed 'battle' between the kings of the earth, who were leaders of the 'wicked', and Yahweh's own faithful servants, the 'righteous ones' led by the Davidic King himself.

Psalm 149 is of particular interest in this part of the festival, because it describes the situation immediately preceding the mimed battle. Yahweh's faithful servants are requested to be ready and prepared, sword in hand, to assist in his victory over the rebellious kings and nations of the earth. Verse 5 f. reads:

Let the faithful exult in glory; let them sing for joy on their couches.

Let the high praises of God be in their throats and two-edged swords in their hands,

To wreak vengeance on the nations and chastisement on the peoples,

To bind their kings with chains and their nobles with fetters of
        iron,
To execute on them the judgement written!
This is glory for all his faithful ones. Praise the Lord!

Then immediately following, and just before dawn, the
'battle' begins. Yahweh's followers fight well, they are out-
numbered but they are not afraid for:

God is our refuge and strength, a very present help in trouble.
Therefore we will not fear though the earth should change,
though the mountains shake in the heart of the sea; though its
waters roar and foam, though the mountains tremble with its
tumult.

                                                    (*Ps.* 46, vv. 1–3).

Nevertheless, Yahweh's faithful ones are gradually overcome, and at last the Davidic King himself is captured and
humiliated by his enemies. Perhaps the enemy leaders in the
mime stripped the king of his regalia, at this stage no doubt he
was made to lie in an undignified position at the feet of his
enemies. The congregation find this situation incredible and are
full of horror at what is happening before their eyes:

But now thou hast cast off and rejected, thou art full of wrath
        against thy anointed.
Thou hast renounced the covenant with thy servant; thou hast
        defiled his crown in the dust.
Thou hast breached all his walls; thou hast laid his stronghold in
        ruins.
All that pass by despoil him: he has become the scorn of his
        neighbours.
Thou hast exalted the right hand of his foes; thou hast made all his
        enemies rejoice.
Yea thou hast turned back the edge of his sword, and thou hast not
        made him stand in battle.
Thou hast removed the sceptre from his hand, and cast his throne
        to the ground.

Thou hast cut short the days of his youth; thou hast covered him
with shame.

> (*Ps.* 89, vv. 38–45)

Now, as the flickering torches are extinguished one by one,
the King himself from his abject position on the ground,
crownless, and stripped of all his royal dignity, pleads with
Yahweh for deliverance:

How long, O Lord? Wilt thou hide thyself for ever?
How long will thy wrath burn like fire?
Remember O Lord what the measure of life is, for what vanity
thou hast created all the sons of men!
What man can live and can never see death?
Who can deliver his soul from the powers of Sheol?

> (*Ps.* 89, vv. 46–8)

By this time the whole scene is in darkness, and only the
voice of the King is heard. He continues to plead with Yahweh,
calling on him to remember his promise of steadfast love for his
people and for the Davidic King who is their representative:

Lord, where is thy steadfast love of old, which by thy faithfulness
thou didst swear to David?
Remember, O Lord, how thy servant is scorned; how I bear in my
bosom the insults of the peoples, with which thy enemies taunt,
O Lord, with which they mock the footsteps of thy anointed.

> (*Ps.* 89, vv. 49–51)

At last when the atmosphere has become almost unbearable
in its intensity, Yahweh *does* come to deliver his people. He
comes at dawn, symbolized by the sun the supreme source of
light and life, and is victorious over the powers of darkness
and death, i.e. the kings and nations of the earth who are the
enemies in the mime. Daylight and Yahweh bring new life to
the faithful ones; the tables are turned and the forces of darkness
and death are overcome in the ritual drama as the sun overcomes

darkness. At this there is a great shout from the congregation:

> God is in the midst of her (Zion), she shall not be moved;
> God will help her right early.
> The nations rage, the kingdoms totter; he utters his voice, the
>   earth melts.
> The Lord of hosts is with us; the God of Jacob is our refuge.
>
> (*Ps.* 46, vv. 5–7)

Now the Temple singers call the congregation to witness the final stages of this great happening, the victorious King speaks in Yahweh's name, and then the whole assembly joins in a great shout of victory:

> Come, behold the works of the Lord, how he has wrought desola-
>   tions in the earth.
> He makes wars cease to the end of the earth; he breaks the bow,
>   and shatters the spear, he burns the chariots with fire!
> 'Be still and know that I am God. I am exalted among the nations,
>   I am exalted in the earth!'
> The Lord of hosts is with us; the God of Jacob is our refuge.
>
> (*Ps.* 46, vv. 8–11)

(*c*) Yahweh's power and might having been established symbolically in ritual mime, and the Davidic King having been delivered from his (and Yahweh's) enemies and accepted as Yahweh's 'son' after pleading his loyalty to Yahweh's Covenant, all is now ready for the triumphal 'victory' procession through the streets of Jerusalem and the enthronement of the Davidic King, as Yahweh's vicegerent in the Temple. Accordingly a great and splendid gathering would assemble outside the city walls. This gathering would consist of musicians and singers who would lead the procession together with the Ark, the symbol of Yahweh's presence. The King himself, now dressed in all his regal splendour, may either have been stationed immediately before or immediately after the Ark (the activities of David himself in a similar procession are recalled by this feature – David in fact 'danced *before* the Lord with all his might' when he brought up the Ark from Obededom to Jerusalem. It is also interesting to note that he was 'girded with a linen ephod' – *2 Sam.* 6: 14). Groups of musicians and singers would no doubt be stationed in different places in the procession, and it is likely that the vanquished 'kings' and 'nations of the earth' also occupied a special place, suitably attired and guarded. Once the procession was on its way round the outside walls there would be a great tumult of noise – the music being interrupted from time to time for the Temple choirs to extol Yahweh's praises and to drive home in the form of a 'question and answer' chant, the character of the worship which is to follow and the character of the worshippers themselves:

> The earth is the Lord's and the fulness thereof, the world and those who dwell therein;
> For he has founded it upon the seas, and established it upon the rivers.
> V. Who shall ascend the hill of the Lord? And who shall stand in his holy place?
> R. He who has clean hands and a pure heart, who does not lift up his soul to what is false, and does not swear deceitfully.
> He will receive blessing from the Lord, and vindication from the God of his salvation.
> Such is the generation of those who seek him, who seek the face of the God of Jacob.
>
> (*Ps.* 24, vv. 1–6)

[handwritten margin note: antiphonal singing]

The procession reaches the city gates, where it comes to a halt. The gates are shut, and there is a shout from the ranks of Israelites standing still in procession:

> Lift up your heads, O gates! and be lifted up, O ancient doors! that the King of glory may come in.
>
> (*Ps.* 24, v. 7)

But their fellow-countrymen on the inside must have the pass-word before they will open the gates and let the procession through. We can imagine how everyone must have listened in silence for the familiar question:

Who is the King of glory?

(*Ps.* 24, v.8a)

The answer has been shown in ritual combat, moreover does not Yahweh himself stand waiting symbolized by his holy Ark, and is not Yahweh's anointed one, the Davidic King there also? A tremendous shout goes up this time:

The Lord, strong and mighty, the Lord, mighty in battle!

(*Ps.* 24, v. 8b)

The keepers of the gates are still not satisfied, however, it is as if they are saying 'Shout louder, we cannot hear you!' So the request to open the gates is repeated from the processional side and the password once more demanded from the inside. This time there is a veritable tumult as the pass-word is bellowed as loudly as each member of the procession can make it:

The Lord of hosts, he is the King of glory!

(*Ps.* 24 v.10b)

The great gates are opened and the Ark, the Davidic King and Yahweh's faithful followers and servants pass on to the Temple itself, where the final act of enthronement takes place.

Once more, as regards the detail of the enthronement itself, there is little direct evidence to be found in the Old Testament books. What is certain, however, is that this New Year Festival did in fact end with the enthronement of the Davidic King, who in his own enthronement signified the enthronement of Yahweh as King over his faithful people, and over the 'kings' and 'nations' of the earth, thus inaugurating once again a new era of righteousness, peace and prosperity. That there was a cult-ritual for this enthronement is certain, and we find that there is a special group of psalms which were very likely the cult-lyrics which accompanied the ritual. The principal psalms in this group are *Psalms* 95–100 and it is noticeable that much of their content is concerned with Yahweh's enthronement as King over his people, the rebellious 'kings' and 'nations' of the earth, primeval chaos, and other gods and godlings, in fact, the psalms contain all the elements which the earlier cult drama contain, they are, as it were, a *reprise* of the cult drama.

In a way, it is perhaps easier to imagine the events of the enthronement than any other part of the New Year Festival, in that it must have contained elements similar to those of our own coronations. There would be much festal music, instrumental and sung, the latter extolling the King's praises (remembering that it is Yahweh in the person of the Davidic King who is really being extolled). There would be much richness of ceremony and vesture, in fact the whole ceremony would be a continual feast of majestic activity culminating in the triumphal moment when the Davidic King was symbolically crowned, with all the people joining together for the great shout of enthronement – 'Yahweh is King'. *Psalm* 29 was probably one of the cult-lyrics, and we can see from this how Yahweh's kingship was extolled, then the congregation shouting aloud in homage as in the person of the Davidic King, he sits enthroned in his holy temple, giving sure strength to his people and the assurance of prosperity and peace during the new era which has just begun:

Ascribe to the Lord, O heavenly beings, ascribe to the Lord glory and strength.
Ascribe to the Lord the glory of his name; worship the Lord in holy array.
The voice of the Lord is upon the waters; the God of glory thunders, the Lord upon many waters.
The voice of the Lord is powerful, the voice of the Lord is full of majesty.
The voice of the Lord breaks the cedars, the Lord breaks the cedars of Lebanon.

He makes Lebanon to skip like a calf, and Sirion like a young wild ox.

The voice of the Lord flashes forth flames of fire. The voice of the Lord shakes the wilderness, the Lord shakes the wilderness of Kadesh.

The voice of the Lord makes the oaks to whirl, and strips the forest bare; and in his temple all cry, 'Glory'

The Lord sits enthroned over the flood; the Lord sits enthroned as king for ever.

May the Lord give strength to his people!

May the Lord bless his people with peace!

As already mentioned (p. 36), the city of Jerusalem eventually fell to Nebuchadnezzar, King of Babylonia, in 586 B.C. This downfall and the resultant destruction of the Temple, brought to an end those elements in the cultic ritual in which the Davidic King had played so important a part. Yet another consequence of Nebuchadnezzar's victory was that the special relationship between King and priesthood also came to an end – indeed these were just two of the many far-reaching changes in the religious life and institutions of Israel brought about by this event. When the Temple was rebuilt and consecrated in 515 B.C. it is likely that priests and singers were re-established there in much the same orders as had existed in pre-exilic times. However, 'the tribal relic of the Ark no longer existed; all that remained was the holy place which it had formerly occupied and which retained its unique significance as a place of worship. Israel remained gathered round it as a religious community, in the narrower circle of those who had remained in the homeland or had returned thither, and in the wider circle of the Diaspora. This led to the priestly element in Israel acquiring an importance which it had not had hitherto' (Martin Noth, *op. cit.*, p. 315). By about 380 B.C., the worship of the new Temple at Jerusalem '. . . was increasingly based on the punctilious fulfilment of existing regulations – the "law of the God of Heaven" which Ezra had brought with him had no doubt included provisions for regulating public worship – and it thereby lost something of the unselfconscious "rejoicing before Yahweh" of which the deuteronomic law had still spoken in stereotyped terms' (*ibid.* pp. 340–1). Jesus' encounters with the religious leaders of his day show us just how much this legalism had developed.[1] As for the New Year Festival, it still kept its place in the scheme of worship, together with the two other ancient feasts of pre-exilic times. Its observance now, though, was a matter of tradition and as a reminder of the exodus from Egypt (see p. 32), its former splendour was obscured, and even its significance as the beginning of the New Year had been taken over by the increasingly important 'Day of Atonement' which was celebrated five days before it (see *Lev.* 23: 27–32 – 'On the tenth day of this seventh month is the day of atonement; it shall be for you a time of holy convocation, and you shall afflict yourselves and present an offering by fire to the Lord. And you shall do no work on this same day; for it is a day of atonement, to make atonement for you before the Lord your God. For whoever is not afflicted on this same day shall be cut off from his people. You shall do no work: it is a statute for ever throughout your generations in all your dwellings. It shall be to you a sabbath of solemn rest, and you shall afflict yourselves; on the ninth day of the month beginning at evening, from evening to evening shall you keep your sabbath').

[1] Cf. amongst many others, the controversy concerning Jesus' healing of the man with dropsy on the Sabbath Day – *Luke*, 14: 1–6.

CHAPTER THREE

The Temple Prophet

ONCE IT WAS REALIZED THAT MANY OF THE PSALMS
are best understood as parts of the text of cultic dramas or
national liturgies used in the assemblies and festivals of Israel,
new ideas began to emerge concerning other aspects of the Old
Testament. The most important of these new ideas involved
the prophets.

The part which the Old Testament prophets played in the
life of God's chosen people is universally recognized as a
highly important one and this importance is indicated in the
Old Testament books by the large amount of writing which
either relates to or stems directly from prophetic activity.
Hence, stories such as Elijah's great triumph over the prophets
of Ba'al (*1 Kings* 18: 17 ff.), or Elisha's healing of Na'aman the
Syrian leper (*2 Kings* 5), are a familiar part of the heritage of Old
Testament history and literature which we have all met. In such
stories the prophets are revealed as the great national heroes of
their day, the fearless, outspoken and often awe-inspiring
champions of Yahweh. It is noticeable already, that the place
of these early prophets is related to that of the king and that
of the priest, and this prophet – priest – king relationship
is a continually recurring one throughout the whole of
the Old Testament. What new light is thrown on it by the

cultic interpretation of the psalms which has already been outlined?

Before answering this question, it is important to call to mind the place of the prophets in the Old Testament historically, remembering that owing to the differing attitudes taken by writers of the historical books towards their source material, it is rather difficult to sort out the exact state of affairs. As with features of the New Year Festival, so it is possible to see in Old Testament prophecy, the development in Israel of an institution which was already in existence in countries surrounding it prior to the gradual conquest of Canaan by the Israelites (*c.* 1200 B.C. onwards). S. H. Hooke writes, 'The existence of such a class of sacred persons attached to the temples, is well attested for the neighbouring countries at a date prior to the entry of Israel into Canaan' (*op. cit.*, p. 146). In the Old Testament itself there is mention of ecstatic prophecy at the very early time of the wanderings in the wilderness (*c.* 1225 B.C.) – 'So Moses went out and told the people the words of the Lord; and he gathered seventy men of the elders of the people, and placed them round the tent. Then the Lord came down in a cloud and spoke to him, and took some of the spirit that was upon him and put it on the seventy elders; and when the spirit rested upon them, they prophesied' (*Num.* 11: 24–5). Later, in the period of the Judges (*c.* 1200 B.C.), the prophetic activity of Deborah is recorded – 'Now Deborah, a prophetess, the wife of Lappidoth was judging Israel at that time. She used to sit under the palm of Deborah between Ramah and Bethel in the hill country of Ephraim; and the people of Israel came up to her for judgement' (*Jud.* 4: 4–5). However it is Samuel who bridges the gap between the rather shadowy history of the Judges and the more exact details of the period of the kings of Israel and Judah. Indeed it is he 'to whom Hebrew tradition assigned the establishment of the prophetic order as a recognized element in the religion of Israel' (S. H. Hooke, *loc. cit*). At any rate Samuel's activities make three things clear:

1. He was a 'Seer'. That is, he was what might today be described as clairvoyant. He offered sacrifices at the local 'High Place' (a shrine usually on top of a hill or situated at the highest point in the neighbourhood) and gave information about lost property for a small fee! An example of Samuel's activities in this last respect is to be found in *1 Samuel*. Saul's father had lost some asses and Saul and a servant were sent to find them. After travelling a considerable distance without any success in their search, Saul says to his servant – 'Come, let us go back, lest my father cease to care about the asses and become anxious about us' (*1 Sam*. 9: 5). The servant however is not willing to give up the search so easily and suggests that they might inquire of Samuel – 'Behold, there is a man of God in this city, and he is a man that is held in honour; all that he says comes true. Let us go there; perhaps he can tell us about the journey on which we have set out' (v. 6). Saul however is still not persuaded, 'But if we go,' he says, 'what can we bring him? For the bread in our sacks is gone, and there is no present to bring to the man of God. What have we got?' (v. 7). His servant replies, 'Here, I have with me the fourth part of a shekel of silver, and I will give it to the man of God, to tell us the way' (v. 8). This is done, and Saul in addition to recovering the lost asses, is also hailed as the future king of Israel and later anointed by Samuel – an action of great significance, as will be seen later on.

2. He was connected with a group of like-minded men who went around prophesying and who were noted for their 'ecstasy' i.e. unusual behaviour, sometimes of a wild nature with possible incoherence. Such a group met Saul a short time after the occasion described above – 'When they (i.e. Saul and his servant) came to Gibeah, behold, a band of prophets met him; and the spirit of God came mightily upon him, and he prophesied among them. And when all who knew him before saw how he prophesied with the prophets, the people said to one another, "What has come over the son of Kish? Is Saul also

among the prophets?"' (*1 Sam.* 10: 10–11). Samuel is recorded as having organized these men into prophetic guilds with centres of activity at well-known local shrines (see *1 Sam.* 19: 18 ff. – 'Now David fled and escaped and he came to Samuel at Ramah, and told him all that Saul had done to him. And he and Samuel went and dwelt at Naioth. And it was told to Saul, "Behold David is at Naioth in Ramah"'). The conclusion of this particular incident indicates something of the form which prophetic ecstasy sometimes took. After sending relays of messengers to capture David, who themselves were overcome by the spirit and prophesied, Saul went himself to Naioth, 'And he too stripped off his clothes, and he too prophesied before Samuel, and lay naked all that day and all that night' (*1 Sam.* 19: 23b–24a).

3. Samuel's activities in relation to Saul and David make very clear the close relationship which was to exist continually between successive generations of prophets and kings right down to the last days of the monarchy in Jerusalem (586 B.C.). It would seem that neither Saul nor David were kings until Samuel had anointed them. The anointing of Saul has already been mentioned (page 50). In David's case, Samuel 'interviewed' each of Jesse's sons in turn until Yahweh told him that he was speaking to the right one – 'Then Samuel took the horn of oil, and anointed him in the midst of his brothers; and the spirit of the Lord came mightily upon David from that day forward' (*1 Sam.* 16: 13). The details of the activities of both kings also indicate that Samuel occupied a position of great authority as their adviser and as the medium through which Yahweh's will was made known to them. After Samuel's death, the prophet Nathan occupies a similar position in David's court and it is he who in company with the priest Zadok, obeys David's instructions to anoint Solomon king – 'King David said, "Call to me Zadok the priest, Nathan the prophet and Benaiah the son of Jehoiada". So they came before the king. And the king said to them, "Take with you the servants of

your lord, and cause Solomon my son to ride on my own mule, and bring him down to Gihon; and let Zadok the priest and Nathan the prophet there anoint him king over Israel; then blow the trumpet and say, Long live King Solomon!"' (*1 Kings* 1: 32–4). This point is an important one because it seems that as a result, prophets were attached officially to the King's court and to the temple, and they were consulted before any major decision, national or private, was taken. An excellent example of this kind of prophecy is the story of how the court prophets Zedekiah and Micaiah prophesied in front of Jehoshaphat, King of Judah, and Ahab, King of Israel, concerning the advisability of them joining together in battle against the King of Syria (*1 Kings* 22: 1–28). A group of court and temple prophets were established in Jerusalem also. Jeremiah obviously did not think very highly of these, for he writes – 'In the prophets of Samaria I saw an unsavoury thing: they prophesied by Ba'al and led my people Israel astray. But in the prophets of Jerusalem I have seen a horrible thing: they commit adultery and walk in lies; they strengthen the hands of evildoers, so that no one turns from his wickedness; all of them have become like Sodom to me, and its inhabitants like Gomorrah' (*Jer.* 23: 13–14).

It can be seen then, that the description 'prophet' as applied to someone in either the united kingdom under Saul, David or Solomon, or in the divided kingdoms of Israel or Judah, could mean one of three things since we can distinguish three quite separate kinds of prophet. First there is the prophet who was a member of one of the prophetic guilds; such prophets are not usually referred to by individual names but by the collective title 'the prophets' or 'a band of prophets'. An example here is *1 Sam.* 10: 10 – 'When they came to Gibeah behold, a band of prophets met him.' Then there is the court or temple prophet like Nathan (see *2 Samuel* 7: 1–3 and numerous other references). Lastly there are the great individual prophets like Amos, or Isaiah, men who for the most part were originally members of the prophetic guilds, but who possessed great personal gifts and who stand out in the Old Testament records as champions of Yahweh, owing allegiance to his voice alone. Such prophets were '. . . the most trenchant critics of the religious institutions of their time, kings, princes, priests and prophets, all alike coming under the lash of their denunciation' (S. H. Hooke, *op. cit.*, p. 148).

So much then for the prophets themselves and their place in Old Testament history. Now what has all this to do with the cultic interpretation of the psalms? It is true to say that much of what has been written about the prophets of Israel in the first half of the present century has been concerned with the contribution made by the prophets to Israel's *understanding* of Yahweh. Of course Israel's understanding of Yahweh did advance very largely as a result of the insight of the prophets over several centuries, and something of this progress can be traced in the prophetic books. Even in them, however, the character of Yahweh is most commonly reflected in some action which he is going to take, or in some judgement which he has carried out in the world, or again in the kind of behaviour which he wants to see among his people. So it is wrong to think that the prophets were deliberately trying to build up a systematic theology. Nevertheless, in the long run, it is in them that the growing awareness and understanding of Yahweh can be traced. What has not been traced, though, and indeed has seldom been studied, is the influence of the prophets on the *worship* of Yahweh, and this may well be equally important. Quite early in the century, however (actually in 1914), a German writer named Hölscher suggested that there were prophets who stood beside the priests in the local and national shrines and who belonged to the staff of these shrines.[1] Once this suggestion has been made, there is plenty of supporting evidence for it in the Old Testament. The 'guilds' of the prophets in ancient Israel were normally connected with the central or a local shrine, and each shrine would have its priest. It was natural that when the temple was built in

[1] The book was entitled *Die Profeten*.

Jerusalem there should be an order of temple prophets there too, and in fact there is evidence which confirms this – *Jeremiah* 29: 26 for instance, refers indirectly to the fact that the temple prophets were under the direction of a priest named Jehoiada. Much later, after the exile in Babylon and in the time of Nehemiah (*c.* 440 B.C.) reference is made to prophets who live under special rules and whose centre of activity is the temple (see *Neh.* 6: 10 ff.). It is also worth noting that both Elijah and his enemies the prophets of Ba'al offer sacrifice, the surrounding detail of this occasion giving no indication that there is anything special in a prophet offering sacrice (*1 Kings* 18: 20 ff.).

Once this mutual relationship and sphere of activity of temple priest and temple prophet is established, some interesting questions present themselves, the most important being 'What exactly was the function of the temple prophet?' Here are some suggestions which have been made which directly concern the place of the prophet in the religious activity of the local shrines and the temple itself.

There were many occasions in the history of Israel when things were not going at all well for God's chosen people. Perhaps they were about to go into battle or were in the middle of one. Or perhaps they had been defeated in battle or were engaged in battle of another kind – against drought or famine. On occasions such as these, a national day of fasting would be proclaimed, and it was natural that the people should all meet together in the temple to beseech Yahweh's aid and to lament the troubled circumstances in which they found themselves. Often on these occasions special observances were called for in addition to fasting – the people were required to abstain from anointing themselves with oil, for instance, or from sexual intercourse. It was also customary for them to tear their clothing, to put on sackcloth, to cover their heads with dust and ashes; all of these actions being outward observances of lamentation and of penitence in Yahweh's sight. Yet other visible activities such as the pouring of water and animal sacrifice continued the idea of penitence, whilst loud weeping, wailing and sighing were a vocal expression of it. One example of many such, is the account of the battle between Israel and the Benjaminites. The former had been crushingly defeated in the first meeting with their enemies:

> Then all the people of Israel, the whole army, went up and came to Bethel and wept; they sat there before the Lord, and fasted that day until evening, and offered burnt offerings and peace offerings before the Lord (*Jud.* 20: 26).

Generally speaking, the symbolic acts at such gatherings are swept up in the form of a prayer of lamentation, spoken sometimes by the King himself, sometimes by priest or prophet. When the Moabites and Ammonites came against Jerusalem (*c.* 850 B.C.) Jehoshaphat, King of Judah, proclaimed a fast throughout the land then called an assembly in the temple and prayed to Yahweh:

> O Lord God of our fathers, art thou not God in heaven? Dost thou not rule over all the kingdoms of the nations? In thy hand are power and might, so that none is able to withstand thee. Didst thou not, O our God, drive out the inhabitants of this land before thy people Israel, and give it for ever to the descendants of Abraham thy friend? And they have dwelt in it, and have built thee in it a sanctuary for thy name, saying, 'If evil comes upon us, the sword, judgement or pestilence, or famine, we will stand before this house, and before thee, for thy name is in this house, and cry to thee in our affliction, and thou wilt hear and save.' And now behold, the men of Ammon and Moab and Mount Se'ir, whom thou wouldest not let Israel invade when they came from the land of Egypt, and whom they avoided and did not destroy – behold they reward us by coming to drive us out of thy possession, which thou hast given us to inherit. O our God, wilt thou not execute judgement upon them? For we are powerless against this great multitude that is coming against us. We do not know what to do, but our eyes are upon thee (*2 Chron.* 20: 6–12).

It is not unreasonable to suppose that in the course of time,

these laments and prayers became formalized as psalms, and
that when occasion presented itself, such psalms became the
basic expression of those attitudes of penitence, lamentation,
hope and trust which were the natural outcome of the particular
circumstances. A regular pattern appears to be followed in
many such psalms and the full outline is shown in the following
example (*all* psalms do not of course reveal the complete
pattern):

(*a*) The people in the case of a communal lament, or the King
or an individual, begin the lament by calling upon Yahweh to
hear them:

> O God, do not keep silence; do not hold thy peace or be still, O
> God!
>
> (*Ps.* 83, v. 1)

(*b*) Yahweh is then praised:

> Give ear, O Shepherd of Israel, thou who leadest Joseph like a
> flock!
> Thou who art enthroned upon the cherubim, shine forth before
> Ephraim, and Benjamin and Manasseh.
>
> (*Ps.* 80, vv. 1–2)

(*c*) The cause of the lamentation is stated:

> Hast thou not rejected us O God?
> Thou dost not go forth O God with our armies.
>
> (*Ps.* 60, v. 10)

(*d*) The prayer is made:

> Turn again O God of Hosts!
> Look down from heaven, and see; have regard for this vine, the
> stock which thy right hand planted.
> They have burned it with fire, they have cut it down; may they
> perish at the rebuke of thy countenance!
>
> (*Ps.* 80, vv. 14–16)

(*e*) An appeal is made to Yahweh's honour:

Help us O God of our salvation, for the glory of thy name;
Deliver us, and forgive our sins for thy name's sake.

(*Ps.* 79, v. 9)

(*f*) The congregation express their humility in Yahweh's sight:

Do not remember against us the iniquities of our forefathers;
Let thy compassion come speedily to meet us, for we are brought
    very low.

(*Ps.* 79, v. 8)

(*g*) They state their confidence that Yahweh will in fact hear them:

Then we thy people, the flock of thy pasture, will give thanks to
    thee for ever;
From generation to generation we will recount thy praise.

(*Ps.* 79, v. 13)

(*h*) Yahweh's merciful answer to the prayer is given in the form of an oracle by a temple prophet:

'Because the poor are despoiled, because the needy groan.
I will now arise,' says the Lord; 'I will place him in the safety for
    which he longs.'
The promises of the Lord are promises that are pure, silver refined
    in a furnace on the ground, purified seven times.

(*Ps.* 12, vv. 5–6)

In view of this basic form or parts of it appearing in different psalms, and especially the recurrence of the same kind of prophetic utterances as those indicated in (*h*) above, it has been suggested that it was more likely the cult prophet who took a leading role on such occasions rather than the cult priest. This view has resulted in some interesting ideas about *2 Isaiah*, for instance. It was thought at one time, that the writer of the psalms must have copied some of his 'salvation promises' from the prophecies in *2 Isaiah*. This would have been a reasonable suggestion had it been based on true assumption that the psalms were written by someone who had searched through Israel's literature collecting the best items for a 'book' of psalms! Such a view however is demonstrably false, and taking into account the fact that so much more is known about the origins of the psalms than before, and in particular about prophetic connection with such origins, it is now considered likely that in fact *2 Isaiah* owes much to the psalmist rather than vice-versa. An example of basic similarity of language and thought is:

> But you, Israel, my servant, Jacob whom I have chosen, the off-spring of Abraham my friend; you whom I took from the ends of the earth, and called from the farthest corners, saying to you 'You are my servant, I have chosen you and not cast you off'; fear not, for I am with you, be not dismayed, for I am your God; I will strengthen you, I will help you, I will uphold you with my victorious right hand. Behold, all who are incensed against you shall be put to shame and confounded; those who strive against you shall be as nothing and shall perish. You shall seek those who contend with you, but you shall not find them; those who war against you shall be as nothing at all. For I, the Lord your God hold your right hand; it is I who say to you, 'Fear not, I will help you' (*Isa.* 41: 8–13).

with:

> Remember the wonderful works that he has done, his miracles, and the judgements he uttered, O offspring of Abraham his servant, sons of Jacob, his chosen ones! For he remembered his holy promise, and Abraham his servant (*Ps.* 105, vv. 5–6; 42).

There are many more examples which could be taken to illustrate the existence and activity of the temple prophets, for the promises which they spoke in Yahweh's name were not simply confined to times of lamentation. In fact they played a

prominent part in the regular festivals also, and in particular
on the occasion of the king's enthronement or at his wedding,
or at the New Year Festival itself. *Psalm* 110, for example, is
clearly a prophetic promise on the occasion of the king's enthronement, and considered alongside the extremely valuable
account in *1 Kings* 1: 33 ff. of the two principal parts of this
festival, the anointing and the actual enthronement, provides us
with a picture of events which went something like this: The
king, sitting on his royal mule moves in procession to the
temple where he dismounts and is led to a high platform in
view of the whole congregation. There he is anointed by a
seer-priest (cf. *1 Sam.* 16: 1 ff.; *1 Kings* 1: 32 ff.) that is, the crown
is placed on his head and the decree, the restatement of Yahweh's Covenant with David, is spoken by a temple prophet.
Psalm 2, vv. 7-9 illustrates this:

> I will tell of the decree of the Lord: He said to me, 'You are my
> son, today I have begotten you. Ask of me and I will make the
> nations your heritage, and the ends of the earth your possession.
> You shall break them with a rod of iron, and dash them in pieces
> like a potter's vessel.'

Amid great rejoicing, singing and shouts of acclamation, the
king is led to Yahweh's throne. This stood in the temple itself,
flanked by winged lions, and symbolized Yahweh's invisible
presence. During the procession, the temple choir sings of the
events which have taken place – the clothing in the holy robe
which the king wore on this occasion; his bathing in the water
from the holy spring of Gehon, and the procession itself:

> Your people will offer themselves freely on the day you lead your
> host in holy array.
> From the womb of the morning like dew your youth will come
> to you.

(Ps. 110, v. 3)

Then just as the king is about to ascend the throne, a temple prophet proclaims the oracle, extolling him as Yahweh's vice-gerent and as the rightful heir to the priest-kingdom of Melchizedek, and giving him the assurance of Yahweh's never-failing presence especially in battle:

> The Lord has sworn and will not change his mind,
> 'You are a priest for ever after the order of Melchizedek.'
>
> (*Ps.* 110, v. 4)

Finally, the king speaks himself to his people, taking up the oracle which the temple prophet has spoken and using it as his 'authority' for sitting on the throne. He then tells the people what he intends to do as king.

Just as the 'answers' to laments became formalized into psalms, so the prophetic oracles and the king's enthronement speech also became psalmody. *Psalm 2* is an excellent example of this latter part of the enthronement festival. The king speaks from his throne against imaginary foreign nations who are contemplating rebellion:

> The kings of the earth set themselves, and the rulers take counsel
>   together against the Lord and against his anointed,
> Saying, 'Let us burst their bonds asunder, and cast their cords
>   from us.'
>
> (*Ps.* 2, vv. 2–3)

He warns them that their plots are doomed to failure because Yahweh has set *him* (the king) on the throne in Zion:

> He who sits in the heavens laughs; the Lord has them in derision.
> Then will he speak to them in his wrath, and terrify them in his
>   fury, saying,
> 'I have set my king on Zion, my holy hill.'
>
> (*Ps.* 2, vv. 4–6)

The proof of this lies in the words which the temple prophet has just spoken and the king repeats the oracle:

I will tell of the decree of the Lord: He said to me,
'You are my son, today I have begotten you. Ask of me and and I
will make the nations your heritage, and the ends of the earth your
possession.
You shall break them with a rod of iron, and dash them in pieces
    like a potter's vessel.'

(Ps. 2, vv. 7–9)

So the rebellious kings are warned that what they really ought
to do is forget all thoughts of rebellion and turn to honour
Yahweh instead:

Now therefore O Kings, be wise; be warned O rulers of the
earth.
Serve the Lord with fear, with trembling kiss his feet, lest he
be angry, and you perish in the way; for his wrath is quickly
kindled.
Blessed are all who take refuge in him.

(Ps. 2, vv. 10–11)

A final example of the activity of the cult prophet was the
offering of general intercessions on behalf of the people. Stories
from the early history of Israel make clear that the prophet was
always regarded as a man of prayer, and that such prayer was
considered very powerful indeed. (cf. *Jer.* 37: 3 ff. where King
Zedekiah sends messengers to Jeremiah asking him for prayers
in time of difficulty – 'King Zedekiah sent Jehucal the son of
Shelemiah and Zephaniah the priest the son of Maaseiah to
Jeremiah the prophet, saying, "Pray for us to the Lord our
God"'.) The illustrations given above of the prophet's part
in pronouncing Yahweh's answer to prayers of lamentation,
etc., suggest that he might also have been responsible for
actually reciting the lamentations in the first place, in much
the same way, perhaps, as intercessions in religious services
today are frequently led by priest or minister with the people
joining in a supplicatory refrain or repeating petitions in litany
form.

Hence, by the side of the psalms used on royal occasions such as *Psalm* 110 and *Psalm* 2 above, there are also psalms which are thoroughly prophetic in character and which would have been used on special occasions, such as the New Year Festival, to express to the faithful king and people, Yahweh's promises of happiness, well-being, victory, fertility, and many other blessings. Such a psalm is *Psalm* 89, part of which was used in the preceding chapter to illustrate the humiliation of the king in the New Year Festival ritual. But note how the tone of this psalm suddenly changes – it becomes packed with prophetic promises of Yahweh's steadfast love and faithfulness, of assurance of victory and blessing. And all this follows exactly the same type of royal oracle which has just been outlined above!

> Of old thou didst speak in a vision to thy faithful one and say 'I have set the crown upon one who is mighty, I have exalted one chosen from the people.
> I have found David, my servant; with my holy oil I have anointed him; so that my hand shall ever abide with him, my arm also shall strengthen him.
> The enemy shall not outwit him, the wicked shall not humble him.
> I will crush his foes before him and strike down those who hate him.
> My faithfulness and my steadfast love shall be with him, and in my name shall his horn be exalted.
> I will set his hand on the sea and his right hand on the rivers.
> He shall cry unto me, "Thou art my Father, my God and the Rock of my salvation."
> And I will make him the first-born, the highest of the kings of the earth.
> My steadfast love I will keep for him for ever, and my covenant will stand firm for him.
> I will establish his line for ever and his throne as the days of the heavens.
> If his children forsake my law and do not walk according to my ordinances,
> If they violate my statutes and do not keep my commandments,

then I will punish their transgression with the rod and their iniquity
with scourges;

But I will not remove from him my steadfast love, or be false to
my faithfulness.

I will not violate my covenant, or alter the word that went forth
from my lips.

Once for all I have sworn by my holiness, I will not lie to David.

His line shall endure for ever, his throne as long as the sun before
me.

Like the moon it shall be established for ever; it shall stand firm
while the skies endure (vv. 19–37).

Of course there are also many psalms of intercession which are
quite simply straightforward intercessions on ordinary occasions. One such is *Psalm* 20 – a psalm which would have been
prayed before a battle, and which promises king and people
Yahweh's help followed by certain victory over their enemies.
This psalm is particularly interesting because of the striking
prophetic element which it contains, and for the way in which
the intercession gradually changes from being a prayer for help
to being a strong prophetic assurance that the prayer has in fact
been answered, and that the answer promises victory:

The Lord answer you in the day of trouble!

The name of the God of Jacob protect you!

May he send you help from the sanctuary, and give you support
from Zion!

May he remember all your offerings, and regard with favour your
burnt sacrifices!

May he grant you your heart's desire, and fulfil all your plans!

May we shout for joy over your victory, and in the name of our
God set up our banners!

May the Lord fulfil all your petitions!

Now I know that the Lord will help his anointed; he will answer
him from his holy heaven with mighty victories by his right hand.

Some boast of chariots, and some of horses; but we boast of the
name of the Lord our God.

They will collapse and fall; but we shall rise and stand upright.

Give victory to the king, O Lord; answer us when we call.

These examples of the place of the temple prophet in Israelite history as revealed by contemporary psalm study, have shown how much more there really was to the prophet's role in temple ritual and worship than has hitherto been realized. Indeed, it is not overstating the case to see the prophet as having a status in the temple at least equal to, and perhaps on occasions even greater than that of the priest.

CHAPTER FOUR

_____

*The New Understanding and the Old:
Cultic Interpretations and Traditional
Interpretations Compared*

IT IS ALREADY OBVIOUS THAT OUR NEW KNOWLEDGE OF
the cultic background of Israel has made striking changes in
our understanding of the psalms. Just how striking these
changes are is going to be shown by comparing the explanation
of some psalms as given by their cultic interpretation, with the
explanation given by some of the more traditional commentators. Incidentally, this comparison will bring out more aspects
of the cult – what really happened at the festivals. Of course,
all the psalms do not fit into the festival pattern, and trying to
make them do so is perhaps one of the greatest dangers of this
new approach. However it is possible to select a group of
psalms which clearly illustrate aspects of the festival pattern
which has already been outlined (see pp. 37 ff., Chapter Two). The
selections are not meant to be exhaustive – they simply consist
of psalms which are in themselves the most important examples
of each aspect. In the outline below, the number of the psalm in
question is given, together with the first line as it is in the
Revised Version of the Bible.

1. General background information concerning the festival

Psalm 72 – "Give the King thy judgements O God'.

The king's place in the social order as 'ruler' or 'judge'; responsible to Yahweh for his own 'righteousness' and that of his people.

Psalm 132 – 'Lord remember for David'.

The Covenant made between Yahweh and the House of David.

Psalm 29 – 'Give unto the Lord O ye sons of the mighty'.

Yahweh is king over the whole of the natural world and he makes his people certain definite promises.

Psalm 95 – 'O come let us sing unto the Lord'.

The people on their part, have equally definite obligations to Yahweh.

2. Aspects of Yahweh's kingship over Israel and the world

Psalm 24 – 'The earth is the Lord's and the fulness thereof.'

Yahweh is hailed as the divine king in all his universal, sovereign power.

Psalm 48 – 'Great is the Lord, and highly to be praised'.

Yahweh triumphs over 'death'.

Psalm 97 – 'The Lord reigneth; let the earth rejoice'.

Through Yahweh, his righteous people also triumph over 'death'.

3. The place of the Davidic King in the festival ritual

Psalm 84 – 'How amiable are thy tabernacles, O Lord of hosts'.

The Davidic King as the 'shield' and 'suffering Messiah.'

Psalm 101 – 'I will sing of mercy and judgement'.

The Davidic King pleads his loyalty to the Covenant and affirms his own and the people's 'righteousness'.

Psalm 18 – 'I love thee O Lord my strength'.

The Davidic King offers thanksgiving for Yahweh's answer to his prayers.

4. *The enthronement of the Davidic King as Yahweh's vicegerent on earth.*

Psalm 2 – 'Why do the nations rage'.

The enthronement of the Davidic King and his endowment with universal power.

Psalm 21 – 'The king shall joy in thy strength O Lord'.

The king is given 'life' and is enthroned. Yahweh's people are assured of his triumph.

First of all then, there are some four psalms which illustrate important background features of the New Year Festival.

Psalm 72 – the king's place in the social order as 'ruler' or 'judge', responsible to Yahweh for his own and the people's 'righteousness'.

This is a psalm which would almost certainly have been declaimed by a temple prophet when the king, having defeated his 'enemies' in the ritual combat, and having taken his place in the resultant 'victory' procession, is now symbolically enthroned in the temple. Its whole tone is one of prayer that the king, who has been given Yahweh's 'justice' and 'righteousness', might exercise the same qualities in reigning over Yahweh's people. It indicates 'the king's supremely important place in the social order' (A. R. Johnson, *op. cit.*, p. 6), and portrays 'almost every aspect of the demands, promises and requirements associated with the king' (S. Mowinckel, *He That Cometh*, p. 80 f):

> Give the king thy justice, O God, and thy righteousness to thy
> royal son!
> May he judge thy people with righteousness, and thy poor with
> justice!   (vv. 1–2)

On such a great and impressive occasion, it is natural that the temple prophet should extend his praise and honour of the king, and acclaim him as a universal monarch also:

> May he have dominion from sea to sea, and from the river (i.e. the Euphrates) to the ends of the earth!
> May his foes bow down before him and his enemies lick the dust!
> May the Kings of Tarshish and of the isles render him tribute, may the kings of Sheba and Seba bring gifts!
> May all kings fall down before him, all nations serve him!
>
> (vv. 8–11)

But the essential point is that the king is, above all else, guardian of the poor and needy, and his right guardianship will lead to economic prosperity:

> For he delivers the needy when he calls, the poor and him who has no helper.
> He has pity on the weak and needy, and saves the lives of the needy.
> From oppression and violence he redeems their life; and precious is their blood in his sight.
> Long may he live, may gold of Sheba be given to him!
> May prayer be made for him continually, and blessings invoked for him all the day!
> May there be abundance of grain in the land; on the tops of the mountains may it wave;
> May its fruit be like Lebanon; and may men blossom forth from the cities like the grass of the field!
> May his name endure for ever, his fame continue as long as the sun!
> May men bless themselves by him, all nations call him blessed!
>
> (vv. 12–17)

To compare this explanation with the interpretation of this psalm given by the older commentaries, we will use Kirkpatrick's *The Psalms* (Cambridge Bible, 1902) and Barnes's *The Psalms* (Westminster Commentary, 1931). Both of these writers see this psalm as a retrospective memory of the glory of Solomon's imperial greatness. Kirkpatrick, in fact, considers that its primary aim is to 'depict the blessings which flow from the righteousness of Yahweh's earthly representative, the theocratic king' (*op. cit.*, p. 416). Hence, although the king for whom it was written must remain uncertain, he suggests that it does refer to some actual king of Judah. Nevertheless, he states, the whole tone of the psalm goes beyond this primary reference in giving a Messianic prophecy of the Kingdom of God on earth in its ideal character of perfection and universality. Barnes, on the other hand, does not make any reference to a particular king, but interprets the psalm as a backward- and forward-looking vision of a seer at a time when Israel was in a state of 'servitude, poverty and misery' (*op. cit.*, p. 342).

The completely different outlooks of the cultic writers and the older traditional commentators is thus made clear right at the outset, and it will be further seen that there are only a very limited number of instances where the two views are at all harmonious.

Psalm 132 – The Covenant made between Yahweh and the House of David.

This psalm is undoubtedly one of the psalms which is closely linked with the New Year Festival and which is specifically connected with the final act of enthronement and the subsequent 'victory' procession through the streets of Jerusalem (see Chapter Two, pp. 42 ff.). Such an event naturally calls to mind the initial transportation of the Ark to Jerusalem from Kiriath-Jearim (v. *1 Sam.* 6. 1; 7. 2), and this historical occasion is duly recounted together with an historical reappraisal of its significance. The psalm falls into two parts: the first is hymnal in character and asks Yahweh's continued favour towards the royal house:

Remember O Lord, in David's favour, all the hardships he endured;

How he swore to the Lord and vowed to the Mighty One of Jacob,
'I will not enter my house or get into my bed; I will not give sleep
to my eyelids, until I find a place for the Lord, a dwelling place for
the Mighty One of Jacob'.
Lo, we heard of it in Ephrathah, we found it in the fields of Jaar.
'Let us go to his dwelling place; let us worship at his footstool!'
Arise O Lord, and go to thy resting place; thou and the ark of thy
   might.
Let thy priests be clothed with righteousness, and let thy saints
   shout for joy.
For thy servant David's sake, do not turn away the face of thy
   anointed one.

(vv. 1–10)

Verse 8, 'Arise O Lord . . . might' is noteworthy, because it
expresses the action taking place at that precise moment as the
Ark is returned to its place in the temple, following the procession round the city.

Then, secondly, there is a vocal response of assurance to the
plea 'For thy servant David's sake do not turn away the face of
thy anointed one'. It is possible that this response was sung
antiphonally by the temple choirs, or simply intoned by a
temple prophet in the form of the usual oracle (see Chapter
Three, p. 60):

The Lord sware to David a sure oath from which he will not turn
   back:
'One of the sons of your body I will set on your throne.
If your sons keep my covenant and my testimonies which I shall
   teach them, their sons also for ever shall sit upon your throne.'
For the Lord has chosen Zion; he has desired it for his habitation:
'This is my resting place for ever; here will I dwell, for I have
   desired it.
I will abundantly bless her provisions; I will satisfy her poor with
   bread.
Her priests will I clothe with salvation and her saints will shout
   for joy.
There will I make a horn to sprout for David; I have prepared a
   lamp for my anointed.

His enemies I will clothe with shame, but upon himself his crown
will shed its lustre'.

(vv. 11–18)

Verse 13, 'For the Lord has chosen Zion; he has desired it for
his habitation', is of special significance. Jerusalem was already
a holy city before it was captured by David. It has been argued[1]
that David found there a Jebusite cult, with a developed ritual
and royal-priestly order of Melchizedek, a 'ritual and mythology
which might prove to be the means of carrying out Yahweh's
purposes for Israel and fusing the chosen people into a model of
national righteousness' (Johnson, *op. cit.*, p. 46). If this is so, then
the origins of the psalm may lie very far back in the history of
the festivals.

Kirkpatrick is quite definite that this psalm is 'an encouragement to the Israel of the Restoration (i.e. 500 c. B.C.), to believe
that Yahweh will not fail to perform his promises to the House
of David' (*op. cit.*, p. 763). Expressing doubts as to the precise
period to which the psalm belongs, he nevertheless favours the
age of Nehemiah. Barnes also considers the psalm to be a
'backward look' by the psalmist to the days of David. Both
commentators discount any suggestion that the dating could be
monarchic – mainly on the grounds that the psalm reads, 'Lord
remember David'.

Psalm 29 – Yahweh is king over the whole of the natural
world, and he gives his people certain definite promises.

This is one of the great enthronement psalms which have
already been touched upon in a previous chapter (see Chapter
Two, p. 45) and which marked the climax of the New Year
Festival, viz. the actual enthronement of the Davidic King as
Yahweh's vicegerent. A. R. Johnson notes that this psalm is a
close parallel, both in language and form, with Ugaritic literature
of the second millennium B.C. The similarities are in fact so great,

[1] A. R. Johnson – *Sacral Kingship in Ancient Israel* (Univ. of Wales Press 1955.
Revd. ed. 1967)

that the psalm 'has been described as in origin a hymn to Ba'al which has been but slightly revised in terms of Yahwism' (*op. cit.*, p. 54). W. F. Albright states that the psalm 'swarms with Canaanitisms in diction and imagery' (*Studies in O.T. Prophecy*, p. 6). Accordingly, Johnson believes that it is possible that the psalm is actually a hymn from the early Jebusite cultus which was adapted to the worship of Yahweh after the city had been captured by David.

The psalm begins with an instruction to the 'godlings' in heaven (an early and primitive concept), to honour Yahweh as supreme:

> Ascribe to the Lord O heavenly beings (godlings), ascribe to the
>   Lord glory and strength.
> Ascribe to the Lord the glory of his name; worship the Lord in
>   holy array.
>
> (vv. 1–2)

The main section then described Yahweh in terms of the Lord of nature, speaking with a mighty voice, whilst in his temple all the people are shouting aloud and praising him:

> The voice of the Lord is upon the waters; the God of glory
>   thunders, the Lord upon many waters.
> The voice of the Lord is powerful, the voice of the Lord is full of
>   majesty.
> The voice of the Lord breaks the cedars, the Lord breaks the
>   cedars of Lebanon.
> He makes Lebanon to skip like a calf, and Sirion like a young wild
>   ox.
> The voice of the Lord flashes forth flames of fire.
> The voice of the Lord shakes the wilderness, the Lord shakes the
>   wilderness of Kadesh.
> The voice of the Lord makes the oaks to whirl, and strips the
>   forests bare; and in his temple all cry 'Glory'.
>
> (vv. 3–9)

Finally the Davidic King sits enthroned as Yahweh's repre-

sentative on earth, and a new era of prosperity and peace has
been inaugurated:

> The Lord sits enthroned over the flood; the Lord sits enthroned
> as king for ever.
> May the Lord give strength to his people! May the Lord bless his
> people with peace!

(vv. 10–11)

Kirkpatrick bases his interpretation on the Greek title of the
psalm in the Septuagint, and therefore holds that it was a
special psalm which was sung in the Second Temple (that is,
from 516 B.C. onwards), on the eighth or concluding day of the
Feast of Tabernacles. To him it expresses the typical devout
Israelite's view of nature, namely, that nature expresses the
beneficence, power and majesty of Yahweh who is supreme
ruler of the universe. Barnes dates the psalm as pre-exilic (i.e.
before 597 B.C.) and it is particularly interesting in the light of
modern interpretations, that he should state specifically (*op. cit.*
p. 142 f):

(i) That the psalm was not originally written for use in public
worship, and

(ii) That "the modern interpretation 'holy garments' in verse
2b is unsuitable to the context."

Psalm 95 – The people, on their part, have equally definite
obligations to Yahweh.

The 'Venite' may well have been sung as a cult lyric, either at
the beginning or end of the New Year Festival (see Chapter 2,
p. 38 f.) as its main theme of Yahweh's power and might as seen
in his creation of the world and in historic events, would be
suitable in either place. In response to the exhortations of the
cult prophet, and in view of Yahweh's covenant promise to be
their shepherd, a solemn charge is given to the worshippers not
to be disobedient to Yahweh as their fathers were in the wilderness:

O that today you would hearken to his voice!

Harden not your hearts, as at Meribah, as on the day of Massah in the wilderness, when your fathers tested me, and put me to the proof, though they had seen my work.

For forty years I loathed that generation and said, 'They are a people who err in heart, and they do not regard my ways.'

Therefore I swore in my anger that they should not enter my rest.

(vv. 7c–11)

Psalm 99 incidentally, follows up the history of the covenant relationship as far as the monarchy, and the establishment of the Ark in Jerusalem:

Moses and Aaron were among his priests, Samuel also was among those who called on his name.

They cried to the Lord, and he answered them. He spoke to them in the pillar of cloud; they kept his testimonies, and the statutes that he gave them.

O Lord our God thou didst answer them; thou wast a forgiving God to them, but an avenger of their wrong-doings.

Extol the Lord, and worship him at his holy mountain; for the Lord our God is holy! (vv. 6–9)

Kirkpatrick treats this psalm as a part of the group *Psalms* 95–100, and is of the opinion that each of these psalms was definitely liturgical, and was probably composed for the Dedication of the Second Temple in 516 B.C. (again he places great weight on the Septuagint titles). Thus it is really the delivery from Babylon, culminating in the Dedication of the Temple, which the psalmist is concerned with here. Barnes simply considers the psalm to be a psalm of 'Ascent' i.e. one of the hymns sung by pilgrims on their way to worship in the Temple.

So far we have been considering the psalms which seem to relate to the main section of the festival drama. In the next group, the psalms selected concern various aspects of the kingship of Yahweh as it was celebrated in the cult.

Psalm 24 – Yahweh is hailed as Divine king in all his universal, sovereign power:

The earth is the Lord's and the fulness thereof, the world and those
   who dwell therein;
For he has founded it upon the seas, and established it upon the
   rivers.

(vv. 1–2)

The importance of this psalm in the cult has already been
stated at length (see Chapter Two, pp. 43 f.). Kirkpatrick com-
menting on it, comes remarkably close to the contemporary cultic interpretation in his suggestion that the 'ancient doors' are the
'gates of the fortress now opening to receive their true Lord'
(*op. cit.*, p. 127), and that the occasion is an actual procession
through Jebus with the Ark as its centre of interest. In his desire
to pin this event down to a definite occasion, he selects the event
of David's installation of the Ark in Jebus following his capture
of the city (see. *2 Sam.* 6). Barnes notes the references to Yahweh's
victory over the 'Deep' and his foundation of the world upon
the 'Floods', and makes a nàtural connection between these and
similar references in the Old Testament narratives of the
Creation.

Psalm 48 – Yahweh triumphs over 'death'.

Here is a dramatic dialogue which might have found its
place in the latter part of the New Year Festival, immediately
before the 'victory' procession. It summarizes, in dialogue
form, the events which have taken place up to this point in
the ritual. The psalm opens with praise – Yahweh is king in
Zion:

Great is the Lord and greatly to be praised in the city of our God!
His holy mountain, beautiful in elevation, is the joy of all the
   earth, Mount Zion, in the far North, the city of the great
   King.

(vv. 1–2)

Then the manner in which Yahweh (actually the Davidic
King in the ritual drama) has been victorious over the kings of
the earth *in Zion* is described:

Within her citadels God has shown himself a sure defence.
For lo, the kings assembled, they came on together.
As soon as they saw it they were astounded, they were in panic,
they took to flight; trembling took hold of them there, anguish as
of a woman in travail.
By the east wind thou didst shatter the ships of Tarshish.

(vv. 3-7)

The people have watched this ritual combat and have seen
for themselves what the outcome has been. They shout in
chorus:

As we have heard, so have we seen in the city of the Lord of hosts,
    in the city of our God, which God establishes for ever.
We have thought on thy steadfast love, O God, in the midst of thy
    temple.

(vv. 8-9)

Yahweh, victorious over 'death' (symbolized in the ritual
drama by the 'kings' and 'nations' of the earth), is further
acclaimed:

As thy name O God, so thy praise reaches to the ends of the
earth.
Thy right hand is filled with victory, let Mount Zion be glad!
Let the daughters of Judah rejoice because of thy judgements.

(vv. 10-11)

Finally the 'cue' for the beginning of the victory procession is
given in the form of a ritual instruction by a temple prophet:

Walk about Zion, go round about her, number her towers, consider well her ramparts, go through her citadels; that you may tell
the next generation that this is God, our God for ever and ever.
He will be our guide for ever.

(vv. 12-14)

Both Kirkpatrick and Barnes are agreed that this psalm is one
of thanksgiving for a great deliverance, its theme being the
greatness of Yahweh and the glory of the city. As to the

occasion, both take it as referring directly to the miraculous deliverance of Jerusalem from the army of Sennacherib in the reign of Hezekiah (in 701 B.C. See *2 Kings* 18: 13 ff.).

Psalm 97 – Through Yahweh, his righteous people also triumph over 'death'.

This is yet another enthronement psalm which is thoroughly cultic in its character and content. It begins with a statement of Yahweh's enthronement in the person of the Davidic King, following the cult battle in which his enemies, the forces of 'darkness' and 'death' have been defeated. The details of the drama in this instance indicate that real fire – probably burning torches – were used in the ritual drama:

> The Lord reigns, let the earth rejoice; let the many coastlands be glad!
> Clouds and thick darkness are round about him; righteousness and justice are the foundations of his throne.
> Fire goes before him, and burns up his adversaries round about.
> His lightnings lighten the world; the earth sees and trembles.
> The mountains melt like wax before the Lord, before the Lord of all the earth.
> The heavens proclaim his righteousness; and the people behold his glory.
>
> (vv. 1–6)

Yahweh's universal power is then proclaimed:

> All worshippers of images are put to shame, who make their boast in worthless idols; all gods bow down before him.
> Zion hears and is glad, and the daughters of Judah rejoice, because of thy judgements, O God.
> For thou, O Lord, art most high over all the earth; thou art exalted far above all gods.
>
> (vv. 7–9)

A temple prophet now exhorts the worshippers to remember the responsibility which they have as Yahweh's chosen people.

Having been delivered, at dawn, from the powers of 'darkness' and 'death', they in turn must now hate all forces of evil:

> The Lord loves those who hate evil; he preserves the lives of his saints; he delivers them from the hand of the wicked.
> Light dawns for the righteous, and joy for the upright in heart.
> Rejoice in the Lord, O you righteous, and give thanks to his holy name.   (vv. 10–12)

Kirkpatrick assigns this psalm to the period of the return from exile in Babylon (*c.* 520 B.C.), and considers that its purpose was a simple song of thanksgiving for deliverance. Barnes entitles his notes on this psalm 'Another song of coming judgement', and goes on to state, 'the psalmist sees in a vision, the Kingdom of God already present' (*op. cit.*, p. 464).

By now, the reader will be familiar with the general picture of the events of the New Year Festival drama. The place of the king in this drama has already been indicated, but it is worth following out the events in greater detail at this stage, and comparing the comments of Kirkpatrick and Barnes with the cultic interpretation of relevant passages.

Psalm 84 – The Davidic King as the 'shield' and 'suffering Messiah'.

It is likely that this psalm was sung by pilgrims as they met together in the temple precincts for the commencement of the New Year Festival, or alternatively, it may have been used by individual pilgrims as a private intercession. The worshippers had come, in many cases from remote places, to worship at the central shrine on this great festival, so it is not surprising to find that they are emotionally stirred at finding themselves in the temple itself. Hence they sing praise to Yahweh, addressing him as 'Yahweh of Hosts', 'Divine King' and 'Living God':

> How lovely is thy dwelling place, O Lord of hosts!
> My soul longs, yea, faints for the courts of the Lord; my heart and my flesh sing for joy to the living God.

Even the sparrow finds a home, and the swallow a nest for herself,
   where she may lay her young at thy altars, O Lord of hosts,
   my king and my God.
Blessed are those who dwell in thy house, ever singing thy praise!
(vv. 1–4)

The pilgrims are happy too, because they know that after the festival will come the rain:

Blessed are the men whose strength is in thee, in whose heart are
   the highways to Zion.
As they go through the valleys of Baca they make it a place of
   springs; the early rain also covers it with pools.
They go from strength to strength; the God of gods will be seen
   in Zion.

(vv. 5–7)

But the focus of the New Year Festival ritual is the Davidic King who represents Yahweh. He is the 'shield' and the 'anointed one' (i.e. Messiah) of Yahweh. So the pilgrims' thoughts move from Yahweh to his earthly representative:

O Lord God of hosts hear my prayer; give ear O God of Jacob!
Behold our shield, O God; look upon the face of thine anointed!
(vv. 8–9)

Then, having called to mind in prayer and meditation the purpose of his visit, the pilgrim goes on to consider once more the delight and privilege of temple worship:

For a day in thy courts is better than a thousand elsewhere.
I would rather be a doorkeeper in the house of my God than dwell
   in the tents of wickedness.
For the Lord God is a sun and shield; he bestows favour and
   honour.
No good thing does the Lord withold from those who walk
   uprightly.
O Lord of hosts, blessed is the man who trusts in thee!
(vv. 10–12)

Barnes seems very wide of the mark in his estimation of this psalm as one written by 'an anointed person, a king or high priest', whose desire is 'that he may be allowed to go up once more to Zion' but who is unable to do so because of some unstated obstacle (*op. cit.*, p. 403). Kirkpatrick, on the other hand, comes closer to the cultic interpretation by his dating of the psalm as having been written during the monarchy (though not as early as David), and by his understanding of the expression 'thine anointed' as a reference to the reigning monarch.

Psalm 101 – The king, speaking at a point in the ritual drama where he has been temporarily overcome by the forces of 'darkness' and 'death', pleads his loyalty to the Covenant with Yahweh, and affirms his own and the people's 'righteousness'.

> I will sing of loyalty and of justice; to thee O Lord I will sing.
> I will give heed to the way that is blameless. O when wilt thou come to me?
> I will walk with integrity of heart within thy house;
> I will not set before my eyes anything that is base.
> I hate the work of those who fall away; it shall not cleave to me.
> Perverseness of heart shall be far from me; I will know nothing of evil.
> Him who slanders his neighbour secretly I will destroy.
> The man of haughty looks and arrogant heart I will not endure.
> I will look with favour on the faithful in the land, that they may dwell with me; he who walks in the way that is blameless shall minister to me.
> No man who practises deceit shall dwell in my house; no man who utters lies shall continue in my presence.
> Morning by morning I will destroy all the wicked in the land, cutting off all the evildoers from the city of the Lord.

Psalm 18 – The Davidic king offers thanksgiving to Yahweh for his answer to prayer.

In this vivid, dramatic psalm, the king speaks of Yaweh's answer to his prayers and of his deliverance from the forces of 'darkness' and 'death'. It is probable that this psalm was an

oration delivered by the king immediately following the ritual
drama of his humiliation by the hostile 'kings' and 'nations' of
the earth and subsequent salvation. He bursts out in praise of
Yahweh:

> I love thee, O Lord, my strength. The Lord is my rock, and my
> fortress, and my deliverer, my God, my rock, in whom I take refuge,
> my shield, and the horn of my salvation, my stronghold.
> I call upon the Lord, who is worthy to be praised, and I am saved
>> from my enemies.
>
> (vv. 1–3)

He goes on to describe the events of his deliverance in vivid
and picturesque language. The details given here suggest that
part of his 'overthrow' might have been his being forced into
the water of the great bronze 'sea' which stood in the temple
forecourt (see Chapter Two, pp. 37 f.):

> The cords of death encompassed me, the torrents of perdition
> assailed me; the cords of Sheol entangled me, the snares of death
> confronted me.
> In my distress I called upon the Lord; to my God I cried for help.
> From his temple he heard my voice, and my cry to him reached his
>> ears. . . .
> He reached from on high, he took me, he drew me out of many
>> waters.
> He delivered me from my strong enemy, and from those who
>> hated me; for they were too mighty for me.
>
> (vv. 4–6; 16–17)

Thus Yahweh's anointed one finds his righteousness vindicated:

> The Lord rewarded me according to my righteousness; according
>> to the cleanness of my hands he recompensed me.
>
> (v. 20)

He then pursues his enemies in the ritual drama, and is victorious over them:

For who is God but the Lord?
And who is a rock except our God? – the God who girded me
   with strength and made my way safe. . . .
I pursued my enemies and overtook them; and did not turn back
   till they were consumed.

(vv. 31–2; 37)

Finally he shouts aloud in a great paean of praise and personal
thanksgiving to Yahweh the 'living' God:

The Lord lives; and blessed be my rock, and exalted be the God of
   my salvation, the God who gave me vengeance and subdued
   peoples under me; who delivered me from my enemies; yea,
   thou didst exalt me above my adversaries; thou didst deliver
   me from men of violence.
For this I will extol thee, O Lord, among the nations, and sing
   praises to thy name.
Great triumphs he gives to his king, and shows steadfast love to
   his anointed, to David and his descendants for ever.

(vv. 46–50)

Kirkpatrick spends a great deal of time on this psalm, elabo-
rating his theory that it was composed by David himself as a
hymn of thanksgiving in the hour of his highest prosperity and
happiness. Having considered the fact that the compiler of *2
Samuel* embodied it in his work as the best illustration of
David's life and character and the noblest specimen of his
poetry (*op. cit.*, p. 85), he dates the composition of the psalm as
'most naturally and fitly assigned to the interval of peace
mentioned in *2 Samuel* 7: 1'. He continues, 'In that time of
tranquillity David reviewed the mercies of Yahweh in this
sublime ode of thanksgiving, and planned to raise a monument
of his gratitude in the scheme for building the temple, which he
was not allowed to carry out'.

Barnes, in an extremely long study of authorship and
evidence, also supports David's authorship, concluding his
study, 'Psalm 18 reveals its religious power in that it has for its
subject the excellencies of a divine protector, but its religion

betrays itself as early and undeveloped by the unmeasured terms in which the fate of the human enemy is described' (*op. cit.*, p. 80).

The final group of psalms for consideration, are concerned with the concluding events of the New Year Festival, namely, the actual enthronement of the Davidic King as Yahweh's representative on earth.

Psalm 2 – The enthronement of the Davidic King and his endowment with universal power.

This psalm is a perfect example of the final stage of the New Year Festival ritual in which the king is enthroned in the temple as Yahweh's vicegerent, following his triumph in the ritual drama over the hostile 'kings' and 'nations' of the earth, which in their turn represent the forces of 'darkness' and 'death'. It is likely that this psalm was spoken antiphonally by the temple choirs, who begin by asking:

Why do the nations conspire, and the people plot in vain?
The kings of the earth set themselves, and the rulers take counsel
    together, against the Lord and his anointed, saying,
'Let us burst their bonds asunder, and cast their cords from us'.

(vv. 1–3)

The answer to this question has already been seen in the ritual drama, so it is proclaimed with triumph:

He who sits in the heavens laughs; the Lord has them in derision.
Then he will speak to them in his wrath, and terrify them in his
    fury, saying,
'I have set my king on Zion, my holy hill.'

(vv. 4–6)

At this point, the king himself, or possibly a temple prophet, recounts an oracle which has been received from Yahweh:

I will tell of the decree of the Lord: he said to me,
'You are my son, today I have begotten you.

Ask of me, and I will make the nations your heritage, and the ends of the earth your possession.

You shall break them with a rod of iron, and dash them in pieces like a potter's vessel.'

(vv. 7–9)

Finally the rebellious 'kings' and 'nations' of the earth who stand by, but now bound captive and utterly defeated, are urged to recognize Yahweh and to show their humility by a ritual act:

Now therefore, O kings, be wise; be warned, O rulers of the earth.

Serve the Lord with fear, with trembling kiss his feet, lest he be angry, and you perish in the way; for his wrath is quickly kindled. Blessed are all who take refuge in him.

(vv. 10–12)

Both Kirkpatrick and Barnes are agreed that the situation presupposed in this psalm is that of an anointed king enthroned on Mount Zion, menaced by a confederacy of subject Gentile nations. In their interpretation of the psalm, however, they put forward different views. Kirkpatrick considers that it could refer to a definite historical occasion, and he is strongly in favour of relating it to the reign of Solomon, although he concludes that 'the particular historical reference is of relatively small moment compared with the typical application of the psalm to the kingdom of Christ' (*op. cit.*, p. 6). Thus he states, 'This psalm is typical and prophetic of the rebellion of the kingdoms of the world against the kingdom of Christ.' Barnes believes that 'it is not Israelite history but Israelite prophecy (or apocalyptic) that harbours the thought of a universal dominion which has its seat in Jerusalem. *Psalm* 2 is not a page from the annals of Israel, but a fragment of a vision of the Kingdom of God' (*op. cit.*, p. 5). Hence his closing sentence, '*Psalm* 2 is a vision of the Holy Catholic Church.'

Psalm 21 – The king is given 'life' and is enthroned. Yahweh's chosen people are assured of his triumph.

This is a psalm very similar in character to *Psalm* 2, and it could have been sung or spoken in antiphonal dramatic form. The opening lines are those of rejoicing, because Yahweh through his assistance to the king in the ritual drama, has granted him the 'life' for which he had earnestly prayed. Victory has in fact been obtained because the king has proved himself loyal and faithful to the covenant relationship:

> In thy strength the king rejoices, O Lord; and in thy help how greatly he exults!
> Thou hast given him his heart's desire, and hast not withheld the request of his lips. . . .
> He asked life of thee; thou gavest it to him, length of days for ever and ever. . . .
> For the king trusts in the Lord; and through the steadfast love of the Most High he shall not be moved.
>
> (vv. 1–2; 4; 7)

The remainder of the psalm honouring the king, directs the worshippers from the ritual combat which they have just seen enacted, to the certainty of victory in real life battle. That is, Yahweh, through his earthly Messiah, will deal with real enemies in the same way as he has dealt with the symbolic enemies of the ritual drama:

> Your hand will find out all your enemies; your right hand will find out those who hate you.
> You will make them as a blazing oven when you appear.
> The Lord will swallow them up in his wrath; and fire will consume them.
> You will destroy their offspring from the earth, and their children from among the sons of men.
> If they plan evil against you, if they devise mischief, they will not succeed.
> For you will put them to flight; you will aim at their faces with your bows.
>
> (vv. 8–12)

The psalm closes with a great shout of praise to Yahweh and the Davidic King:

Be exalted, O Lord, in thy strength!
We will sing and praise thy power.

(v. 13)

Kirkpatrick considers that this psalm is one of thanksgiving for victory and that 'its occasion need not be looked for in a coronation festival or a royal birthday' (*op. cit.*, p. 109 f.). Barnes, whilst accepting the same general view, believes that it is the king's might, not Yahweh's, which is being celebrated. He does, however, show some sympathy towards the suggestion that the psalm was liturgical, and possibly used before a battle, to accompany sacrifice to and invocation of, Yahweh.

The considerable divergence between the interpretation of these selected psalms, by writers steeped in knowledge of the ancient cult liturgies of Israel, and those whose work may be said to be based on an approach which attempted to classify the psalms historically and assign historical dates and events to their contents, has been made abundantly clear. In the chapter which follows, some of the ways in which the cultic approach has been seen to be unsatisfactory, or at best, extreme, will be outlined.

What next? The Cultic Interpretation of the Psalms is developed and questioned

NEW INSIGHTS IN ANY FIELD OF STUDY ALWAYS TEND to create excitement and controversy. The new insights into the interpretation of the psalms which have so far been mentioned have proved to be no exception. Thus, on the one hand, recent years have seen very considerable development of the basic 'cultic' position, and on the other hand, serious questioning of the position itself. In this chapter, therefore, some of the principal ways in which this development has shown itself will be outlined, together with some of the opinions and critical comments of the more noteworthy opponents of the cultic interpretation of the psalms. The reader will then have sufficient information to enable him to form his own opinion as to the value of the cultic approach in his own understanding of the psalter.

So far, there has been no mention in this book, of a group of writers well-known in theological circles, who are usually given the title of the 'Uppsala School'. As the name itself indicates, these writers are all connected with the University of Uppsala in Sweden, a centre which has been responsible for the production of much highly important work based on the study of ancient Israelite cult rituals. Because Uppsala is the centre of activity, it is generally assumed that the writers who belong to the 'school' have a common viewpoint on matters of psalm interpretation. This is not so – in fact the work of these scholars shows that there is a considerable diversity of opinion amongst them. Professor G. W. Anderson has given what is perhaps the best definition of the term. He writes, '. . . for convenience, the term "Uppsala School" may be retained to describe a group of scholars, connected, for the most part, with the old Swedish University, in whose work there is a common emphasis, a common approach and a common *type* of solution, even where there is controversy over detail' (*Harvard Theological Review*, Vol. XLIII, 1950). He goes on to state what this 'common emphasis' and 'common approach' is, namely, that 'In the fields of textual and literary criticism, great emphasis is laid on the importance and reliability of oral tradition. In the study of religion the school is anti-evolutionist, and is concerned to stress the abiding positive influence of the cult, and the importance of the role of both king and prophet in the cult' (*loc. cit*).

It is interesting to note that the cultic approach to the psalms has not yet made its impact on the Western world in anything like so startling a way that it has in Scandinavian countries. As a result, much hard work has been done on ancient Israel's cult liturgies by Scandinavian writers and comparatively little, for instance, by English writers. It is by no means an easy task to present a summary of the work of the Uppsala School. Published studies are mainly to be found in European languages other than English, a fact which does of course account for the comparative slowness of the process of dissemination of cultic ideas on the psalms. Then too, these studies are often of a highly individual nature, so that it frequently becomes difficult to generalize or present overall summaries of the work which has been done. However this is what is obviously needed and an attempt will now be made to indicate some of the general conclusions which have been reached with regard to the cultic activities in Ancient Israel of which the psalms were originally believed to have been a part.

The outline which follows comes from the introduction to Aage Bentzen's *King and Messiah*, a book which *has* been published in English, and which gives a basic illustration of the interpretation of Israel's ancient liturgies upon which more detailed studies have been based. It will be noticed that all the main parts of Israel's ancient New Year Festival which have been traced and indicated already (e.g. in Chapter Three), are to be found again here.

Bentzen describes the festival of Yahweh's enthronement on New Year's Day as a ritual drama, with the re-creation of the world as its central theme. Psalms which are directly related to the festival are again the familiar ones, e.g. *Psalms* 47, 93, 95–100 (the 'enthronement' psalms) and others. In this ritual drama, celebrated at the time of the autumn equinox, the people of Israel experienced a repetition of the events of Creation. This involved Yahweh's battle against the powers of Chaos, the primeval ocean, Rahab the dragon, and all the demonic powers which accompanied them. In this battle, Yahweh is the overwhelming victor, and as a final protection for his people against Chaos, the Seas and the Floods, he builds the heavenly vault. The creation of the heavens, therefore, is a great and decisive act of salvation on Yahweh's part, and proves that he is a supreme power above all Gods:

> For all the gods of the people are idols;
> > but the Lord made the heavens.
>
> > > > > (*Ps.* 96, v. 5)

Through a religious act of 'remembrance', that is a communal act of recollection of ancient events, the people were able to experience afresh Yahweh's great act of salvation, and they once again perceive his assurance of life:

When I look at thy heavens, the work of thy fingers, the moon and
   the stars which thou hast established;
What is man that thou art mindful of him, and the son of man that
   thou dost care for him?
Yet thou hast made him little less than God, and dost crown him
   with glory and honour.

(Ps. 8, vv. 3–5)

Having established the pattern of Israel's ancient cult
liturgy, it was then noticed that the New Year Festival had a
close relationship with similar religious celebrations held in
countries throughout the ancient Near East. In particular, it
was found that the Ras Shamrah tablets, discovered in N. Syria
in 1929 and years following, indicated that a similar kind of enthronement festival was found also in ancient Canaan.

When attention was focused on details of the New Year
Festival, really controversial interpretations began to be put
forward. A specially important consideration was the figure of
the divine or sacral king and his role in the cult. Now the
familiar activity of the Davidic king in the temple ritual has
already been sufficiently illustrated in previous chapters, but it
will be remembered that towards the end of the cult drama he is
temporarily humiliated and overcome by the people in the
drama who represent the forces of evil and death. Then finally,
he is raised up in triumph by Yahweh and thereby shows symbolically Yahweh's assurance of life and salvation for his
people. It is in suggesting that the Israelite New Year Festival
was in essence the same in this respect as that of the surrounding nations, that the Uppsala School has aroused most criticism,
for in addition to the suggestion that some sort of 'divinity' was
ascribed to the king, there is an implication that perhaps
Yahweh himself may have been thought of as a dying and
rising God. This possibility has met with consistent and abso-
lute rejection on the part of more traditional scholars, and
indeed, many studies emanating from Uppsala and other important European centres, have denied this interpretation.

Bentzen writes, 'These ideas were accepted by Israel only in a modified form. The "dying God", as Pedersen, Hvidberg and Engnell unanimously assert, was incompatible with Israel's idea of God. Yahweh was eminently the "Living God", the "God of Life", the God "who does not die" as the original text of *Habakkuk* 1: 12 runs according to rabbinical tradition. But this connection did not prevent certain features from the ritual combat between Yahweh and the powers of Chaos, as we see it in poetical allusions in Job, the Prophets, above all in Deutero-Isaiah, from entering the world of Israelite thought.' Although Bentzen speaks for the vast majority of scholars, it is worth noting that the suggestion that Yahweh might have been thought of as a dying and rising God is not deduced only from the assignment of elements of neighbouring cults to Israel's festival. Professor G. Widengren published a work in 1955 in which he suggested that certain passages from the psalms might be understood as supporting such an interpretation, namely:

> Arise, O Lord, in thy anger, lift thyself up against the fury of my enemies;
> *Awake* O my God; thou hast appointed a judgement.
>
> *(Ps.* 7, v. 6)

and

> The Lord *lives*; and blessed be my rock, and exalted be the God of my salvation.
>
> *(Ps.* 18, v. 46)

By way of complete contrast, Artur Weiser in his recently translated Commentary on the psalms (1962) writes of this second verse, "In the formula 'Yahweh lives", the contrast is expressed with the corresponding phrase in the cults of the dying and rising vegetation Gods' *(The Psalms,* p. 196, footnote)!

There is general agreement that ancient Israel did reinterpret the myth of the battle of the Gods to some extent, and also gave it historical significance. In the Passover ritual, for instance, Yahweh waged war against the 'nations'; the 'chaos', Rahab, and Tiamat the dragon, were identified with the nation of Egypt and the Pharaoh; and the story of the Exodus itself was embellished with features which were originally to be found in the Creation legends. Such features naturally turned up again in the psalms, particularly the 'royal' psalms. Of course, references to the king either directly, or by use of his title 'The Lord's anointed' are not found only in the 'royal' psalms, and this fact led Swedish writers to suggest that such psalms as these have been 'democratized'. This is a term used to indicate a process in which it is assumed that all the psalms originally began their existence as part of a royal ritual, but in course of time these rituals became accessible to and known by the general public. A particular feature of these 'democratized' psalms is their references to the innocent suffering of the servant of God:

My God, my God, why hast thou forsaken me?
Why art thou so far from helping me, from the words of my
    groaning?

(*Ps.* 22, v. 1)

Further interesting discussion has centred around the identity of the 'enemies' in the psalms. Bentzen's conclusions in this respect are fairly typical of the general agreement on this point. Even where the king is not explicitly mentioned, he says, we shall probably have to conclude that the 'enemies' are primarily the power of Chaos, the primeval enemies of men and God, who are conquered by the sacral king. Reinterpretation in a historical context, however, has meant that in some cases the enemies have actually been thought of as the concrete enemies of the nation or the individual – demonic powers, for instance, or men who have made a covenant with such powers, sorcerers perhaps – indeed 'whatever else combats the plans of the saving

God of the Creation story'. A good example of such a psalm is
Psalm 59:

> Deliver me from my enemies, O my God, protect me from those
> who rise up against me, deliver me from those who work evil, and
> save me from bloodthirsty men. . . .
> Each evening they come back, howling like dogs and prowling
>   about the city.
> There they are, bellowing with their mouths, and snarling with
>   their lips – for 'Who', they think, 'will hear us?'
> But thou, O Lord, dost laugh at them; thou dost hold all the
>   nations in derision.
>
>   (vv. 1–2; 6–8)

As these verses sum up all that is hostile to Yahweh, it is easy to
imagine this psalm as having its place in a cultic drama in which
Yahweh's ultimate victory is symbolically represented, his
enemies crushed, and his people assured once more of life. As
long ago as 1933 it was suggested by Birkeland that the
'enemies' in the psalms are usually foreigners, and that the 'I'
who speaks in such passages could therefore be the king, or
perhaps the leader of the army if this is not the king, or in post-
exilic times a native governor or high priest. Birkeland has
reiterated this view in a more recent article, 'The evil-doers in
the Psalms' (*A.N.V.A.O.*, ii., 1955). However the discussion
proceeds, and opinions on this subject are many and varied,
though on the whole Bentzen's summary above is representative of much of contemporary opinion.

    As the work of scholars and writers on the cultic approach to
the psalms is gradually made available to wider circles of
readers, fresh insights are continually being gained into many
other aspects of the psalter. But what of the criticism which has
been offered of the cultic approach itself? Has it shown up any
fundamental weaknesses in the basic assumptions of those who
champion the cause of a cultic interpretation of the psalms?
The simple answer to this question is in the negative, but the

standpoints from which criticism has been levelled are of considerable interest and do give valuable help in clarifying the issues which are at stake. One general criticism of the 'Uppsala School' is that it has pressed the cultic approach to the psalms to an unreasonable and unjustifiable length. A particular instance of development seen in this light is the case already mentioned above of the Davidic King seen as possessing some kind of divinity, and the further implication that as he represented Yahweh in the ritual drama, it is possible that Yahweh himself might have been thought of as a dying and rising God. It is certain that such an interpretation as this is very hard to reconcile with the picture which the Old Testament presents of the God of Israel, and many critics have hastened to point this out. A further ground of criticism of the school, which incidentally comes as much from its supporters as those who are in opposition to its ideas, is that its work reveals a wrong emphasis. Thus, for some critics, the tendency which the school has of placing primary emphasis on external sources such as archaeological findings or the religious observances of countries outside Israel's borders, is putting the cart before the horse. There is indeed a strong argument here that interpretation of the Old Testament should start with the Old Testament itself and work outwards from it to the insights which archaeological research or comparative studies of religion have to offer. In reversing the accepted processes of biblical exegesis the school certainly has laid itself open to charges of 'reading in' conclusions and theories rather than finding these naturally develop out of studies which were soundly based on the biblical text. A. R. Johnson has made the point that it is of the utmost importance to look into all those aspects of man's relationship with Yahweh which can be found in the Old Testament when considering the Israelite conception of kingship. And he goes on to offer a warning that until the position is absolutely clear it is best to avoid such controversial expressions as 'Divine Kingship' in describing the religious status of Israel's kings!

Criticism of specific aspects of the cultic interpretation of the psalms can be found in numerous articles contained in a wide variety of published works, but the most direct criticism in small scale, is contained in an article in *Expository Times*, Vol. LXVIII (1956), p. 144 ff., written by Professor W. F. McCullough of the University of Toronto and entitled 'Israel's Kings, Sacral and Otherwise'. In this article, the author is focusing his attention primarily upon a now standard work by A. R. Johnson (*Sacral Kingship in Ancient Israel*) first published in 1955, but his considerations do have a general application to the field of cultic interpretation as a whole. Considering the Hebrew monarchy, he concludes that the impression which the Old Testament gives of the kings both of Israel and Judah, is that they did not differ very much from kings reigning over the smaller countries which were their neighbours, and that the rite of anointing probably became in course of time a formality, rather than an act which might be interpreted as conveying or implying any 'sacral' character.

As to the place of the king as a religious leader, Professor McCullough agrees that this role was certainly performed by David and Solomon, but he denies that any clear picture can be obtained of the place in the cult of kings who succeeded Solomon. It is only natural that prayers such as those found in the 'Royal' psalms should be offered for the reigning king, but he does not consider that this necessarily invests the king with any sacral status. If this were the case, then it is very surprising that no echoes of the king's sacral state are to be found in the Jewish law.

The biggest portion of Professor McCullough's article is concerned with Israel's autumnal festival. Concurring with the view that there *was* such a festival in Israel, and that aspects of it were the celebration in song and dance of Yahweh's supreme powers in primeval battle, in Creation and in history, (which explains the 'enthronement' psalms, e.g. *Pss.* 96–100), he goes on to deny that Yahweh was in any sense enthroned annually. Nor can he see any valid historical connection between later religious developments in Jerusalem, and the earlier Jebusite cult rituals which were celebrated there before David's time (see Chapter Two, p. 34 f.). As to the existence of a cult drama, he maintains that he has no presuppositions which would make him deny that this had a place in ancient Israel, but if it did, and it was in fact as detailed in character as has been suggested, then it is very surprising that only those few poems which are now to be found in the psalms, have come down in history.

Concluding his article, Professor McCullough discusses numerous technical points of interpretation, the longest consideration being concerned with the place which 'death' had in the thought of ancient Israel. In this connection he strongly denies that the evidence adduced for the king's participation in the cult drama to the point where he finds himself symbolically at the mercy of 'Death' and pleads to Yahweh for deliverance, is at all convincing.

A. R. Johnson, in a short reply to McCullough's article in the same volume of *Expository Times* (p. 178 ff.) indicates that he is in no way disconcerted by it. On the contrary he concludes by expressing his gratitude to McCullough for confirming his own belief that one of the essentials in modern Old Testament study is a 'disciplined imagination'!

There is left one further contributor of note in the field of cultic psalm study, and this is Professor Norman Snaith. As far back as 1934, Dr Snaith produced a book entitled *Studies in the Psalter* in which he endeavoured to show that the psalms which Mowinckel associated most closely with the New Year Festival were really written after the Jews were exiled in Babylon (i.e. later than 537 B.C.), and were in any event, psalms written for use on the Sabbath Day. They could not therefore form the basis for the kind of pre-exilic festival suggested by Mowinckel. In 1947, Professor Snaith produced a second book entitled *The Jewish New Year Festival: its origins and development*, and this volume is noteworthy in that the author, after studying the same myth and ritual patterns which have been outlined in earlier chapters of this book, arrives at highly original conclusions. He considers that in the pre-exilic New Year Festival in Israel, there were two chief aspects – a feast of thanksgiving for the blessing of the Old Year, and a New Year feast of prayer and supplication in which prayers for rain played the main part. After detailed examination of the origin of the Hebrew words 'Chodesh' and 'Shabbath', Dr Snaith interprets the former as 'Full moon day' and the latter as 'New moon day'. He then proceeds to rule out the enthronement psalms (*Pss.* 95–100) as being evidence of the ritual of the New Year Festival, for in his opinion these are not New Year psalms at all but Sabbath psalms and are therefore being misapplied.

In his final chapter, which is probably the one most relevant to the present day cultic position, Dr Snaith considers the importance of the New Year festivals in Mesopotamia and Syria, and their influence on Israel's life and worship. So far as the Babylonian New Year Festival is concerned, he sees this as having a decidedly urban character, and as being closely linked with astrology, whereas the cult of Israel was obviously that of an agricultural people and stressed fertility. It is not surprising, therefore, to find that his conclusion is that the similarities between Hebrew and Mesopotamian rites do not indicate that there was any large scale 'borrowing' either during or after the period of the kings of either Israel or Judah. He states: 'In Syria we have a development along the lines demanded by a predominantly agricultural community, with Tammuz–Adonis associations prevailing. In Mesopotamia the deities tend to be more separate each from the other. They have their astral associations, and a whole world of astrological lore comes to be introduced. On the other hand in Palestine the tendency is for the ancient "mana" ideas to prevail, and also for fertility cults to prevail, especially the weeping for Tammuz (*Ezek.* 8: 14), the cult of creeping beasts (v. 10), the worship of the rising sun' (v. 16).[1] This latter is the type of cultus which shows most traces in the Old Testament, until the time when the kings who were tributary to Assyria and Babylonia introduced the cults of their overlords, but these new ideas were of comparatively late date, and few of them seem to have survived the exile.

The exile itself led to a new contact with Babylon, and the effect of this is to be seen in the new ideas concerning the Sabbath, in a revival of the ancient Rahab-myth (e.g. Second Isaiah), and in such cult innovations as the introduction of incense. But we find no adoption of Babylonian cult ceremonies after the pattern Mowinckel presupposes. The new Israel had a tremendous horror of all such associations, and it is unlikely that any new dramatizations were introduced which in any way allowed the Deity to be represented by mortal man, nor was there any king who could take a role anything approaching that which was demanded of Babylonian kings' (*op. cit.*, p. 220).

Dr Snaith's book is very detailed and scholarly. It indicates many new points of interest, and illustrates by its criticism of certain features of the myth and ritual position, the necessity of a cautious approach in the assessment of the value of new material and theories. Nevertheless, the author's own arguments are by no means conclusive and have not met with either a great deal of acceptance or support.

One particularly interesting aspect of Dr Snaith's position, is that on various occasions throughout his book he assumes that certain passages of the psalms are 'borrowed' from Second

---

[1] The texts read:

Ezek. 8: 14 – 'Then he brought me to the entrance of the north gate of the house of the Lord; and behold there sat women weeping for Tammuz'.

Ezek. 8: 10 – 'So I went in and saw; and there, portrayed upon the wall round about, were all kinds of creeping things, and loathsome beasts, and all the idols of the house of Israel'.

Ezek. 8: 16 – 'And he brought me into the inner court of the house of the Lord; and behold, at the door of the temple of the Lord, between the porch and the altar, were about twenty-five men, with their backs to the temple of the Lord, and their faces towards the east, worshipping the sun towards the east'.

Isaiah (i.e. the writer responsible for Chapters 40–55 of *Isaiah*).
He writes, 'In the case, for instance, of *Psalm* 98. 3b, it is plain
from the Hebrew that we have a transcription from *Isaiah* 52. 10;
and there are many other indications of dependence upon *Isaiah*
40–55' (*op. cit.*, p. 36). The texts in question are:

All the ends of the earth have seen the victory of our God.

(*Ps.* 98, v. 3b)

. . . and all the ends of the earth shall see the salvation of our God.

(*Is.* 52, v. 10b)

The point is that such instances as these are as much evidence
that Second Isaiah 'borrowed' from the psalms in question as
vice-versa! Indeed, one of the foundations of Mowinckel's
position is that the enthronement psalms have in fact influenced
Second Isaiah's style and thought. Mowinckel writes, 'It is not,
as earlier interpreters of the psalms used to think, the character
and style of the enthronement psalms which are modelled on
Deutero-Isaiah as a result of poetic concentration on his sayings, but the other way round; prophecy has here, as is so often
the case, borrowed forms and expressions from cultic lyrics'
(*The Psalms in Israel's Worship*, Eng. trans. D. R. Ap-Thomas.
Vol. I, p. 190). It is this possible duality of interpretation that led
A. R. Johnson to describe Snaith's conclusions as a 'two-edged
sword', a remark which has been taken up by other writers on
more than one occasion since.[1]

It is noteworthy that no new work has been published on the
psalms in recent years which has not devoted a major part to the
formative influences of Israel's ancient cultic liturgies upon
the psalter. A major event of 1962 was the publication in English
translation by D. R. Ap-Thomas, of Mowinckel's *Offersang og
Sangoffer*. Bearing the English title *The Psalms in Israel's Worship*,

[1] See A. R. Johnson's chapter 'The Psalms' – *O.T. & Modern Study* (1951) p.
194. And for recent quotation, Helmer Ringren *The Faith of the Psalmist* intro. p.
xviii (1963).

and reflecting the author's detailed additions and fresh insights since it was first published in 1951, this brought to a very much widened circle of readers all the knowledge and experience gained from a lifetime's study of the psalms. The same year also saw the appearance in English of Artur Weiser's *The Psalms*, a truly monumental work, which in the words of its publishers (S.C.M. Press Ltd) 'is intended to supply the need, often noted, for a full commentary in English, taking into account the many developments which have taken place in the study of the psalms over the last quarter century'. Weiser's commentary is noteworthy in that he gives much attention to the view that in ancient Israel, an important part of the New Year Festival was devoted to the renewal of the covenant between Yahweh and his chosen people Israel. Indeed, he gives the annual New Year Festival itself the title 'Covenant Festival' throughout, and this is indicative of the considerable emphasis placed upon this aspect of the purpose and liturgy of the festival. Thus *Psalm* 50 is taken as a paradigm of the covenant renewal liturgy. In verse 5 of this psalm a direct reference is made by the temple prophet to the covenant established between Yahweh and Moses, the leader of the chosen people, at Sinai (see. *Exod.* 24):

'Gather to me my faithful ones, who made a covenant with me by sacrifice!'

In this reference, initial covenant details are recalled in the minds of the worshippers – details which would be very familiar as part of the narrative of the exodus from Egypt:

'Moses came and told the people all the words of the Lord and all the ordinances; and all the people answered with one voice, and said, "All the words which the Lord has spoken we will do." And Moses wrote all the words of the Lord. And he rose early in the morning, and built an altar at the foot of the mountain, and twelve pillars, according to the twelve tribes of Israel. And he sent young men of the people of Israel, who offered burnt offerings and sacrificed peace offerings of oxen to the Lord. And Moses took half of the blood and put it in basins, and half of the blood he threw against the altar. Then he took the book of the covenant, and read it in the hearing of the people; and they said, "All that the Lord has spoken we will do, and we will be obedient." And Moses took the blood, and threw it upon the people, and said, "Behold the blood of the covenant which the Lord has made with you in accordance with all these words"' (*Exod.* 24, vv. 3–8).

Psalm 50 itself, then, begins with a temple prophet extolling the greatness of Yahweh and proclaiming his divine rule as King and Judge from Zion:

> The Mighty One, God the Lord, speaks and summons the earth from the rising of the sun to its setting.
> Out of Zion, the perfection of beauty, God shines forth.
> Our God comes, he does not keep silence, before him is a devouring fire, round about him a mighty tempest.
> He calls to the heavens above and to the earth, that he may judge his people. (vv. 1–4)

The prophet then declares Yahweh's known will and his name:

> 'Hear O my people and I will speak, O Israel, I will testify against you. I am God, your God.' (v. 7)

He then directs the worshippers to a right state of heart for the covenant renewal itself:

> 'Offer to God a sacrifice of thanksgiving, and pay your vows to the Most High; and call upon me in the day of trouble;
> I will deliver you and you will glorify me.' (vv. 14–15)

Finally the prophet states that Yahweh will judge both the faithful and the wicked worshippers:

> But to the wicked God says: 'What right have you to recite my statutes, or take my covenant on your lips?

For you hate discipline, and cast my words behind you.

If you see a thief, you are a friend of his; and you keep company with adulterers.

You give your mouth free rein for evil, and your tongue frames deceit.

You sit and speak against your brother; you slander your own mother's son.

These things you have done and I have been silent; you thought that I was one like yourself.

But now I rebuke you, and lay the charge before you.

Mark this, then, you who forget God, lest I rend, and there be none to deliver!

He who brings thanksgiving as his sacrifice honours me; to him who orders his way aright I will show the salvation of God!.'

(vv. 16-23)

A last development in modern psalm study is an eminently readable book by Helmer Ringgren, published in 1963.[1] The author, who was himself both student and teacher at the University of Uppsala, has produced in .this work, entitled *The Faith of the Psalmist*, a clear and reasoned assessment of contemporary international discussion of the psalms. This book is highly recommended as an introduction to the cultic approach to the psalms and is particularly useful for readers who may not wish to follow this through in the larger and more detailed commentaries of the day.

[1] S.C.M. Press Ltd., 'Greenback' series.

CHAPTER SIX

Some Questions Answered

IT IS CLEAR THEN, THAT MANY OF THE PSALMS
were written for the ritual of cultic celebrations and national
festivals, and to see them in relation to the drama of the cult is
to understand them far more fully than we were able to from the
older and more traditional viewpoint, which regarded them as
personal poems, often describing particular historical incidents.
Since this cultic interpretation has proved so useful in revealing
the true meaning of many of the most vivid of the psalms, can
it be used as well on all of them, and is the whole psalter to be
seen as a kind of fragmented libretto of the festivals? Or do
there remain psalms in the collection for which no direct connection with the cult can be discovered or suggested?

In the first chapter of this book a general outline was given of
the common views regarding the origin of the psalms, their
date, authorship and titles. In fact, study in these fields can be
most frustrating, because it is virtually impossible to obtain
results which are anything more than conjecture. For instance,
nobody can suggest with any degree of certainty how the
psalter came to be divided into groups or 'books'. It is probable
that this division only came about at a comparatively late date,
perhaps during the second century B.C., and that the reason for
it was a conscious desire to parallel the five-fold division of the

'law' books attributed to Moses. Each so-called psalm book ends with a doxology. Thus:

Book I – *Psalm* 41, vv. 13:

> Blessed be the Lord, the God of Israel, from everlasting to everlasting! Amen and Amen.

Book II – *Psalm* 72, vv. 18–19:

> Blessed be the Lord, the God of Israel, who alone does wondrous things.
> Blessed be his glorious name for ever; may his glory fill the whole earth! Amen and Amen.

Book III – *Psalm* 89, vv. 52:

> Blessed be the Lord for ever! Amen and Amen.

Book IV – *Psalm* 106, vv. 48:

> Blessed be the Lord, the God of Israel, from everlasting to everlasting!
> And let all the people say, 'Amen!' Praise the Lord!

These doxologies were taken to be intended divisions between the respective 'books' and the whole of *Psalm* 150

> Praise God in his sanctuary; praise him in his mighty firmament!...
> Let everything that breathes praise the Lord!

as the doxology of Book V and of the complete psalter. Clearly the doxologies were useful to the person who originally made the five-fold division, but far from being themselves written for this purpose originally, it would seem that they are liturgical additions to the particular psalms of which they form the conclusion. On the whole there is little indication therefore that this five-fold division takes into account any special kind of psalm, and what homogeneity there is in those psalms which can be grouped together specifically, is largely due to a still earlier collection, traces of which can be seen on close examination. For instance, one very interesting indication of an earlier grouping of psalms is the fact that nearly all the psalms in what is known as Book I (i.e. *Pss.* 1–41) use in the original Hebrew text, the word 'Yahweh' for 'God'. However in *Psalms* 42–83, a group which contains psalms classified in the present Books II and III, instead of 'Yahweh' the word 'Elohim' is used for 'God'. Clearly these two quite large collections of psalms used to exist independently at one time, the more primitive probably being the group using 'Yahweh' for 'God'. It is very difficult to speak with any certainty concerning what may have happened here, but it does seem likely that this 'Elohistic' collection was available and being used in the temple at a time when the people did not wish to pronounce the real name of God openly – it is generally assumed that this was a question of reverence. But this does not mean that these psalms were actually written at this time – in fact all the evidence points to the fact that the 'Elohistic' editor actually changed the sacred name all the way through from 'Yahweh', as it was originally in these psalms, to 'Elohim'!

As has already been suggested in the first chapter, the titles of the psalms as we have them, do give some help, albeit only in a very limited way, in picking out psalms which were related to the cult. Perhaps the most notable group of psalms in this connection are *Psalms* 120–34 each of which carries the title 'A song of Ascents'. It has always been considered that these titles indicated their use by pilgrims on their way to worship at the temple – that is, that they were a sort of travelling song collection. Mowinckel points out here that most of these fifteen psalms have nothing to do with pilgrimages, but that they are temple psalms used in the actual festival processions at harvest and New Year. Besides these there are various other titles which might indicate cultic use, such as 'A song of praise' e.g. *Ps.* 145 which begins 'I will extol thee, my God and King, and bless thy name for ever and ever'). Here is a psalm which would suit any part of the cult ritual in which Yahweh was to be extolled as the supreme creator. 'For Penance' is the title of *Psalm* 88 which begins:

> O Lord my God, I call for help by day; I cry out in the night before thee.

This psalm would fit exactly the circumstances of the king's ritual humiliation in the New Year Festival, or the individual's self-humiliation which would be part of his ritual purification say, from illness. Unfortunately once again there is no assurance that the present titles of the psalms are historically reliable, or that they give us any firm indication of the purpose for which any particular psalm was either written or used. If the dates of the psalms could be determined or reliably estimated, it might not be difficult to define the use for which each separate poem was written. But apart from a few psalms which seem to have primitive elements and may be dated in the age of the kings, and others which have affinities with wisdom literature and can be placed as belonging to the post-exilic age, the psalms are difficult to date, and authorities vary widely in their estimates. We cannot draw any firm line between all those which are cultic in character and all those which are not. We can, however, follow Mowinckel in distinguishing some which are in the psalter and have no apparent connection with the festivals; he cites as examples *Psalms* 1, 19b, 34, 37, 49, 78, 105, 106, 111, 112 and 127. These psalms are classified with relative ease into certain defined categories, as they illustrate overall similarities of content and style. Thus *Psalms* 34, 37, 49, 78, 105, 111 and 112 are typical of later 'teaching' instruction about Yahweh and his righteous actions, and they include the authors' beliefs about the destinies of both good and evil people. *Psalm* 112 reads:

> Blessed is the man who fears the Lord, who greatly delights in his commandments!

His descendants will be mighty in the land; the generation of the upright will be blessed.

Wealth and riches are in his house; and his righteousness endures for ever.

Light rises in the darkness for the upright; the Lord is gracious, merciful and righteous.

It is well with the man who deals generously and lends, who conducts his affairs with justice.

For the righteous will never be moved; he will be remembered for ever.

He is not afraid of evil tidings; his heart is firm, trusting in the Lord.

His heart is steady, he will not be afraid, until he sees his desire on his adversaries.

He has distributed freely, he has given to the poor; his righteousness endures for ever; his horn is exalted in honour.

The wicked man sees it and is angry; he gnashes his teeth and melts away; the desire of the wicked man comes to naught.

Sometimes all these characteristics are to be found concentrated into a psalm which has a direct historical association – a 'hymnal legend' as Mowinckel calls it. Such is *Psalm* 78, which like *Psalm* 105 is a synopsis of a part of ancient Israelite history:

Give ear, O my people, to my teaching; incline your ears to the words of my mouth!

I will open my mouth in a parable; I will utter dark sayings from of old, things that we have heard and known, that our fathers have told us.

We will not hide them from their children, but tell to the coming generation the glorious deeds of the Lord, and his might, and the wonders which he has wrought.

He established a testimony in Jacob, and appointed a law in Israel, which he commanded our fathers to teach to their children; that the next generation might know them, the children yet unborn, and arise and tell them to their children. . . .

In the sight of their fathers, he wrought marvels in the land of Egypt, in the fields of Zoan.

He divided the sea and let them pass through it, and made the waters stand like a heap.

In the daytime he led them with a cloud, and all the night with a
fiery light . . .

(vv. 1–6; 12-14)

Another development of this pattern is the psalm in which
Israelite history is used with a strongly penitential character
about it so that the historical detail throws into high relief the
plea for God's mercy and forgiveness for sin: *Psalm* 106 is a
good example of this kind of writing:

O give thanks to the Lord for he is good; for his steadfast love
endures for ever!

Who can utter the mighty doings of the Lord, or show forth all
his praise?

Blessed are they who observe justice, who do righteousness at all
times!

Remember me, O Lord, when thou showest favour to thy people;
help me when thou deliverest them;

That I may see the prosperity of thy chosen ones, that I may
rejoice in the gladness of thy nation, that I may glory with thy
heritage.

Both we and our fathers have sinned; we have committed
iniquity, we have done wickedly.

Our fathers, when they were in Egypt, did not consider thy
wonderful works; they did not remember the abundance of thy
steadfast love, but rebelled against the Most High at the Red Sea.

Yet he saved them for his name's sake, that he might make known
his mighty power.

He rebuked the Red Sea, and it became dry; and he led them
through the deep as through a desert . . .

(vv. 1–9)

An interesting variant on this theme is *Psalm* 19b, where the
writer has taken an ancient hymn to the sun and added to it
a poem in praise of the law of Yahweh, and an expression of
his own zeal for that law. This love of the law, which is also
celebrated superbly in *Psalm* 1, is a constant note of much of the
Wisdom writings. *Psalm* 119 may also be classified as being
similar in content to the latter part of *Psalm* 19 which reads:

The heavens are telling the glory of God; and the firmament proclaims his handiwork.

Day to day pours forth speech, and night to night declares knowledge.

There is no speech, nor are there words; their voice is not heard; yet their voice goes out through all the earth, and their words to the end of the world.

In them has he set a tent for the sun, which comes forth like a bridegroom leaving his chamber, and like a strong man runs its course with joy.

Its rising is from the end of the heavens, and its circuit to the end of them; and there is nothing hid from its heat.

The law of the Lord is perfect, reviving the soul; the testimony of the Lord is sure, making wise the simple;

The precepts of the Lord are right, rejoicing the heart; the commandment of the Lord is pure, enlightening the eyes;

The fear of the Lord is clean, enduring for ever; the ordinances of the Lord are true, and righteous altogether.

More to be desired are they than gold, even much fine gold; sweeter also than honey and drippings of the honeycomb.

Moreover by them is thy servant warned; in keeping of them there is great reward.

Who can discern his errors? Clear thou me from hidden faults.

Keep back thy servant also from presumptuous sins; let them not have dominion over me!

So shall I be blameless, and innocent of great transgression.

Let the words of my mouth and the meditation of my heart, be acceptable in thy sight, O Lord, my rock and my redeemer.

Finally there remain in this group, psalms such as *Psalm* 1 and 127 which seem to be entirely personal in character. In the case of these two psalms, it is likely that they were written by unknown scribes who were themselves involved in the task of making up the Canonical psalter as we know it. It has been suggested that *Psalm* 1 may have been specially written to be the introduction to the whole collection; most commentators, however, think this unlikely. If it is to set the tone of the complete Book of Psalms for the reader (as the final doxology of

Psalms 150 sets the seal on the whole book), then the scribes who edited the final version visualised the pious reader as 'meditating' the texts, or repeating them over and over to himself. Thus *Psalm* 1:

> Blessed is the man who walks not in the counsel of the wicked, nor stands in the way of sinners, nor sits in the seat of scoffers;
> But his delight is in the law of the Lord, and on his law he meditates day and night.
> He is like a tree planted by streams of water, that yields its fruit in its season, and its leaf does not wither.
> In all that he does he prospers.
> The wicked are not so, but are like the chaff which the wind drives away.
> Therefore the wicked will not stand in the judgement, nor sinners in the congregation of the righteous; for the Lord knows the way of the righteous, but the way of the wicked will perish.

Although most commentators are agreed that it is unlikely that this psalm was specially written as an introduction to the psalter, nevertheless it is highly appropriate in this position. *Psalm* 127 is a happy little psalm in which the writer rejoices in his trust in Yahweh, and in his own sons who are Yahweh's gift:

> Unless the Lord builds the house, those who build it labour in vain.
> Unless the Lord watches over the city, the watchman stays awake in vain.
> It is vain that you rise up early and go late to rest, eating the bread of anxious toil; for he gives to his beloved sleep.
> Lo, sons are a heritage from the Lord, the fruit of the womb a reward.
> Like arrows in the hand of a warrior are the sons of one's youth.
> Happy is the man who has his quiver full of them! He shall not be put to shame when he speaks with his enemies in the gate.

In the long run, the new understanding of the psalms must be expected to bring some changes in the ways in which the Church uses them in public worship. One distinctively Christian use of the psalms is likely to remain unchanged: the Christian Church, from New Testament times onwards, has always regarded certain of the psalms, notably the 'royal' psalms, as prophecies of Christ. Early references in the New Testament texts which speak of the disciples' use of the psalms to support their claim that Jesus was the promised Messiah, are a clear proof of this. For instance, *Acts 2*, 34–6 reads:

> For David did not ascend into the heavens; but he himself says, 'The Lord said to my Lord, Sit at my right hand, till I make thy enemies a stool for thy feet.' Let all the house of Israel therefore know assuredly that God has made him both Lord and Christ, this Jesus whom you crucified.

There is a direct quotation used here from *Psalm* 110, v. 1:

> The Lord says to my Lord; 'Sit at my right hand, till I make your enemies your footstool'.

In the light of what has already been said about the ancient Israelite view of the Davidic King as Yahweh's vicegerent, or his 'anointed one', it is not surprising that Jesus' followers were quick to use verses from the psalms as proof texts of his messianic status. In fact the disciples already had Jesus' own example to follow in this respect. In St Mark's Gospel, the plainest and least elaborated of the Gospels, there are numerous occasions when he uses psalm texts in relation to his own mission or person either directly or by implication. In St Mark, Chapter 11, v. 9, Jesus' triumphant entry into Jerusalem is described as follows:

> And those who went before and those who followed, cried out, 'Hosanna! Blessed is he who comes in the name of the Lord! Blessed is the kingdom of our father David that is coming! Hosanna in the highest.'

Here Jesus allows this quotation from *Psalm* 118, v, 26 to be applied to him. The Psalm verse reads:

> Blessed be he who enters in the name of the Lord! We bless you from the house of the Lord.

In St Mark's Gospel, Chapter 12, vv. 10–11, Jesus actually uses a portion of the same *Psalm* 118, by implication, as referring to his own treatment by the Jewish people. The Gospel narrative reads:

> Have you not read this scripture: 'The very stone which the builders rejected has become the head of the corner; this was the Lord's doing, and it is marvellous in our eyes?'

Psalm 118, vv. 22–3 reads:

> The stone which the builders rejected has become the head of the corner.
> This is the Lord's doing; it is marvellous in our eyes.

In the same chapter of St Mark's Gospel, Jesus made use of the very text from *Psalms* 110, v. 1 which St Peter used in Acts 2: 34 and which has already been discussed above. Finally there is one of the most familiar verses from St Mark's passion narrative to look at in this connection. Jesus' own words from the cross echo the opening verse of *Psalm* 22:

> And at the ninth hour Jesus cried with a loud voice, 'Eloi, Eloi, lama sabachthani?' which means, 'My God, my God, why hast thou forsaken me?'

Helmer Ringgren has crystallized the relationship of the psalm quotations discussed here with the Church's use of them as prophecies of Jesus, in these words – 'It has been shown that the Messianic hope in Israel grew out of the idea of the king as the God-sent ruler. The royal psalms prepare the way for the Christian belief in the Messiah, and thus form an important and essential part of the history of revelation. As a matter of fact, the Christian belief in Jesus as the messianic King and Saviour would be unthinkable and unintelligible apart from the background of the Old Testament kingship ideology as expressed in the royal psalms' (*The Faith of the Psalmists*, p. 114).

The 'suffering servant' concept, which it is likely that Deutero-Isaiah himself gained from the psalms, or more likely from the experience of using the psalms in a cultic setting, was also taken over by the Christian Church and related to Jesus. As a result, words which echo *Psalm* 22, v. 18 for instance, are to be found in two of the synoptic gospel accounts of the crucifixion. *Psalm* 22, v. 18 reads:

> They divide my garments among them and for my raiment they cast lots.

This verse may be compared with *Matthew* 27. 35 – 'And when they had crucified him, they divided his garments among them by casting lots' (see also *Luke* 23. 34). And there is a direct quotation of it in St John's Gospel 19. 24: 'So they said to one another, "Let us not tear it (i.e. the seamless robe), but cast lots for it to see whose it shall be." This was to fulfil the scripture, "They parted my garments among them, and for my clothing they cast lots"'.

Quite early on in this book, it was indicated that a good deal of work by scholars in the present century has helped to show that the Old Testament owes much to common factors in the religion of the whole of the ancient Near East. Ancient Israel did not exist in isolation – she shared a common cultural background with her national neighbours, notably Babylon and Egypt. Indeed it is certain aspects of the religion of these two countries, which when followed by Israel herself, led to protests by the great prophets – notably in the field of worship of gods other than Yahweh. A large-scale survey of the work which has been done in this field cannot be made here, but it is worth taking a brief look at both the differences and similarities which come to light when (in particular), specific Babylonian and Egyptian religious texts are compared with the psalms of Israel. At the outset it is also worth keeping in mind Helmer

Ringgren's warning that on the one hand the same expressions, when used in different religious literature, do not always mean the same thing. And on the other hand, that it is extremely difficult to state with any degree of clarity, the exact differences between biblical and non-biblical religion:

When the Old Testament and Babylonian psalms are compared, very close resemblances are found in respect both of the pattern of the psalms and of the imagery used in them. Ringgren cites the following:

Babylonian	*Old Testament*
The wrath of god and goddess is placed upon me.	Thy wrath lies heavy upon me. (*Ps.* 88, v. 7)
How long, O my Lady, wilt thou be angry and therefore thy face be turned away?	How long, O Lord? Wilt thou forget me for ever? How long wilt thou hide thy face from me? (*Ps.* 13, v. 1)
Food I ate not, weeping was my bread, water I drank not, tears were my drink.	My tears have been my food day and night. (*Ps.* 42, v. 3)
Friends and companions rage against me, the people of my city rage against me.	Even my bosom friend in whom I trusted . . . has lifted his heel against me. (*Ps.* 41, v. 9)
He is thrown among the billows of the flood, the deluge has mounted over him, the shore is far off from him. . . he has perished in a deep place.	For the waters have come up to my neck. I sink in deep mire, where there is no foothold; I have come into deep waters, and the flood sweeps over me. (*Ps.* 69, vv. 1–2)
Unloose my sin, loosen my iniquity. Remove my wantonness, loosen my transgression.	Pardon my guilt, for it is great . . . and forgive all my sins. (*Ps.* 25, vv. 11, 18)

The religious content of such writing also reveals strong similarities. Here is a Babylonian psalm, a prayer to the goddess Ishtar, which shows a close affinity to several of the penitential psalms of the Old Testament psalter:

I have cried to thee suffering, wearied, and distressed, as thy
    servant;
See me, O my Lady, accept my prayers.
Faithfully look upon me, and hear my supplication.
Promise me forgiveness, and let my spirit be appeased. . . .
Forgive my sin, my iniquity, my shameful deeds, and my offence,
Overlook my shameful deeds, accept my prayer,
Loosen my fetters, secure my deliverance, guide my steps aright . . .

One of the most famous Egyptian parallels is the hymn to the sun, a poem of the Pharaoh Akhenaton *c.*1350 B.C. It is particularly instructive to notice that whereas the Egyptian poem sees the activities of the Sun (God) as quiescent during the night, the Old Testament writer extends Yahweh's creative purpose to the night as well as to the day:

When thou settest in the western horizon, the land is darkness, in
    the manner of death. . . .
Every lion comes forth from his den; all creeping things, they
    sting.
Darkness is a shroud, and the earth is stillness, for he who made
    them rests in the horizon.

Psalm 104, vv. 20–1 reads:

Thou makest darkness and it is night, when all the beasts of the
    forest creep forth.
The young lions roar for their prey, seeking their food from God.

It is further possible, from some inscriptions which are in the Egyptian temple of Horus at Edfu and of Hathor at Denderah, to find Egyptian passages which show clear affinity with Old Testament psalms which in their turn formed part of the initial liturgy of the New Year Festival, viz.:

O you prophets and priests, all you who enter before the gods. . . .
Do not appear with sin, do not enter in uncleanness, do not speak
    lies in his house!
Do not embezzle the provisions!
Do not collect taxes to the detriment of the poor to benefit the
    rich!
Do not add to the weight and the measure, but reduce them!
Do not do wrong in matters of sacrifices!

Compare *Psalm* 15:

O Lord, who shall sojourn in thy tent? Who shall dwell on thy
    holy hill?
He who walks blamelessly, and does what is right, and speaks
    truth from his heart;
Who does not slander with his tongue, and does no evil to his
    friend, nor takes up a reproach against his neighbour;
In whose eyes a reprobate is despised, but who honours those who
    fear the Lord; who swears to his own hurt and does not
    change;
Who does not put out his money at interest, and does not take a
    bribe against the innocent.
He who does these things shall never be moved.

Lastly, in this short comparison of Israelite and neighbouring
national religious writing, it is of considerable relevance to be
aware of Ringgren's point, that wheareas a Babylonian writer
might address his God using language such as 'Who is like
thee among the Gods?' or 'Thou hast no equal', it is very clear
that he would not here be questioning the *existence* of other
gods. In Israel, on the other hand, the psalms clearly indicate
the exclusiveness of Yahweh, and nowhere is this more evident
than in those psalms which are specially associated with the
New Year or enthronement festival, e.g.:

For all the gods of the peoples are idols; but the Lord made the
    heavens. . . .
Say among the nations, 'The Lord reigns' . . . .

                                            (*Ps.* 96, vv. 5, 10)

There remains one final question which can be a subject for speculation only, namely, Is there a continued place for the psalms in contemporary church life? On the one hand recent years have seen the 'modernization' of the biblical text in such publications as the Revised Standard Version and the Jerusalem Bible, and the Old Testament text in the New English Bible is expected in the not too distant future. These new versions of the Old Testament text have provided us with a much more recognizable and intelligible psalter. The result has been to throw into sharp relief the doubts already expressed by many churchgoers concerning the use and meaningfulness of the psalter in public worship today. There is no new problem here – the 1928 Anglican Prayer Book for instance, sought to exclude some of the more violent passages as being thoroughly contrary to the Christian spirit. An example of such a suggested omission is *Psalm* 68, vv. 21–3:

> But God will shatter the heads of his enemies, the hairy crown of
>   him who walks in his guilty ways.
> The Lord said 'I will bring them back from Bashan, I will bring
> them back from the depths of the sea, that you may bathe your feet
> in blood, that the tongues of your dogs may have their portion
> from the foe'.

and the notoriously imprecatory verses of *Psalm* 137, vv. 7–9:

> Remember, O Lord, against the Edomites the day of Jerusalem,
> how they said, 'Rase it, rase it!
> Down to its foundations!'
> O daughter of Babylon, you devastator! Happy shall he be who
>   requites you with what you have done to us!
> Happy shall he be who takes your little ones and dashes them
>   against the rock!

Of course such thought is completely out of character with Christian worship, but the problem is greater, namely, Is there any place at all for the psalms in Christian worship today as they are essentially the record of *pre*-Christian religious attitude? To this question it is possible to give the answer that many of the psalms do still have valid 'worshipful' content, that is, they could continue to be used in Christian worship, because they express timeless truths about the nature of God or the individual soul, regardless of their pre-Christian origin. Obvious examples of such psalms are the well-loved *Psalm* 23 – 'The Lord is my shepherd I shall not want' or *Psalm* 100 – 'Make a joyful noise to the Lord, all the lands'. Clearly selection would require the appointment of specially convened groups of people within a particular denomination. No doubt, too, a large portion of the present psalter could be retained as a result of such scrutiny, but the more irrelevant historical psalms and those which are sub-Christian, could well be dispensed with.

Even if this selective process did in fact take place and a revised psalter (i.e. revised in content) became available for church use, the complete Old Testament psalms would still retain their place in the Bible. This book began with a quotation from Richard Hooker, the great 16th-century theologian; it is fitting that it should end with the words of Sigmund Mowinckel, a man whose work has made an outstanding contribution in the present century to our understanding of the real-life situation of the psalms. He writes – 'No book of the Old Testament has been read so much throughout the ages as the Book of Psalms, 'the Psalms of David' as they are popularly termed. The sense of the actuality of the prophets has often fluctuated; in evil times, in war, and in great disasters men have felt their significance more easily than under other conditions. But in the psalms the human heart has found its own counterpart at all times, in sorrow and in happiness, as an individual and as a member of God's people' (*The Psalms in Israel's Worship*, Vol. 1, p. 1). This is surely a fitting expression of the high place which the psalms will always hold in the lives of those who have come to know them, and love them, and make them their own.

SELECT BIBLIOGRAPHY

Sacral Kingship in Ancient Israel, A. R. Johnson (Mystic, Conn.: Verry, Lawrence Inc., 1967).

The Faith of the Psalmists, Helmer Ringgren (Philadelphia: Fortress Press, 1963).

The Psalms in Israel's Worship, Vols. I & II, S. Mowinckel, trans. D. R. Ap-Thomas (Nashville: Abingdon Press, 1962).

The Psalms, Artur Weiser, trans. H. Hartwell (Philadelphia: The Westminster Press, 1962).

INDEX OF REFERENCES TO PSALMS